Illustrator:
Bruce Hedges

Editorial Project Manager:
Charles Payne, M.A., M.F.A.

Editor in Chief:
Sharon Coan, M.S. Ed.

Art Director:
Elayne Roberts

Art Coordinator:
Cheri Macoubrie Wilson

Associate Designer:
Denise Bauer

Cover Artist:
Jose Tapia

Product Manager:
Phil Garcia

Imaging:
Alfred Lau
James Edward Grace

Trademarks:
Trademarked names and graphics appear throughout this book. Instead of listing every firm and entity which owns the trademarks or inserting a trademark symbol with each mention of a trademarked name, the publishers aver that they are using the names and graphics only for editorial purposes and to the benefit of the trademarked owner with no intention of infringing upon that trademark.

Publishers:
Rachelle Cracchiolo, M.S. Ed.
Mary Dupuy Smith, M.S. Ed.

Managing Technology In The 1* Computer Classroom

*or two or three

Author:

Susan L. Gimotty, M.A.

Teacher Created Materials, Inc.
6421 Industry Way
Westminster, CA 92683
www.teachercreated.com

ISBN-1-57690-457-1

Reprinted, 1999
Made in U.S.A.

Teacher Created Materials

TABLE OF CONTENTS

TABLE OF CONTENTS *(cont.)*

INTRODUCTION

My involvement with technology was rather accidental. I was fresh out of graduate school, teaching fourth grade at Norfolk Academy in Virginia. I had a head full of knowledge but very little hands-on experience. A few months into the year, my principal asked me to attend a computer seminar. As a first-year teacher trying to make a positive impression on the principal, I said yes! After attending the seminar, I thought I would try a few of the ideas in my classroom with my one computer. Via my Radio Shack computer and a slow, slow 2400 baud modem, I networked with other classes around the country and gathered weather data. My students loved this! I must tell you that my modem was using the same phone line as the main office of the school. So whenever my students and I wanted to use the modem to contact other schools, I would have to send a student to the office to ask the staff to get off the phone!

I then began to attend more technology seminars, and I would try one or two of the ideas in my classroom. I found that the students were motivated and engaged in learning. Isn't this what I had always wanted for my students? A computer revolution had begun in my classroom. Technology has forever changed the way I teach, and I trust that this book, *The One-Computer Classroom*, will empower you to effectively use that one computer in your classroom.

As Technology Director at the Barstow School in Kansas City, I have had the privilege to train a variety of teachers who have entered into the technology age at many different levels. Drawing upon these experiences, I have designed *The One-Computer Classroom* book to empower teachers whether they are new to technology or have been involved for a long time. The first part of *The One-Computer Classroom* discusses connectivity and management with one computer. The next section highlights using the computer as a productivity resource, such as making portfolios, newsletters, memos, and computing grades. In addition, using the computer as a presentation tool for events such as classroom lesson or Back-to-School Night will be explained.

The second part of *The One-Computer Classroom* is devoted to using the computer with the students. The lessons and activities contained in this book will help get you started on all of the different ways you can integrate technology into your current classroom curriculum. You will find lesson plans, templates, and even Internet Web sites to enhance many of the units you already teach. The last part of *The One-Computer Classroom* addresses both skill building and simulation software to use in the classroom with one computer. Several pieces of software which will reinforce a host of skills such as multiplication or phonics will be highlighted. Also, simulation software which enables teachers to take their students to exotic places such as the coral reefs or planet Mars via the computer will be discussed.

The One-Computer Classroom is an excellent resource for classroom teachers looking for ways to use technology to increase their productivity, enhance student learning, and reinforce their curriculum. The goal of this book is to help you become knowledgeable and even confident with the ever-changing technologies facing you as a teacher today. Teachers all over the world are facing these same issues, and I trust this book will give you the tools to embrace this technology.

Note: At the time of this printing all Web sites were accurate. Teacher Created Materials attempts to offset the fickle nature of the Web by posting changes of URLs on our Web site. Check our home page at **www.teachercreated.com** for updates on this book.

WHAT IS HARDWARE?

Often, teachers are given computers with few or no instructions. I will try to avoid all of the "techy" jargon and start with the basics of the computer. Hardware, simply put, is any computer technology that one can touch. The computer, printer, monitor, keyboard, and mouse are all hardware components. These are the tools that carry out the instructions that the software gives them. Your brain, for instance, is the greatest piece of computer hardware known to man. It is a maze of interconnected circuits which carries out instructions that have been loaded through a lifetime of experience. What makes the brain such a perfect piece of hardware is that it is continually being upgraded to process faster and remember things better. Computer hardware, on the other hand, needs to be physically upgraded or even replaced periodically in order to run new or more powerful software.

PLATFORM

Platform refers to the type of computer/operating system. There are two major choices: Windows (IBM-compatible) or Macintosh. In the past, this was a major decision when considering a purchase because historically IBM compatible machines could not run Macintosh programs and vice versa. With the development of hybrid software (software that can run on either type of machine), this problem has become less significant. However, most educators feel it is easier to have the same type of computer at home and work because files will transfer more easily.

FLOPPY DISK DRIVES

The floppy disk drive allows a computer user to save data and programs on removable floppy disks or diskettes. This is particularly important in the one-computer classroom because usually teachers will have students save their work on their personal floppy disks. Remember, disks that are used in the floppy disk drive do not hold as much information as a typical hard drive. So if you are trying to save a file on a floppy disk and the computer says that your disk is out of memory, then you will need to delete items on your disk or locate a second disk. If you are carrying floppy disks from home to school, make sure you keep them in a plastic case. Floppy disks can easily fail, especially if handled improperly.

CD-ROMS

Like a floppy disk, a CD-ROM drive is able to read data and programs that are stored on CD-ROM discs. Most software today comes on a CD-ROM. One advantage of CD-ROMs is that they can hold a great deal of information. Complete encyclopedias have been placed on these discs. They are also able to hold a variety of information such as sound, video, and animation.

It is important for you and your students to understand the parts of the computer. Whether you have a Macintosh or PC, the parts are basically the same. The next two pages contain blackline masters that you can reproduce for your students. One blackline master has the different parts labeled, and one does not. For younger students, you may want them to color and label the parts of the computer on page 7. This project will help familiarize your students with the different hardware pieces and their names.

WHAT IS HARDWARE? *(cont.)*

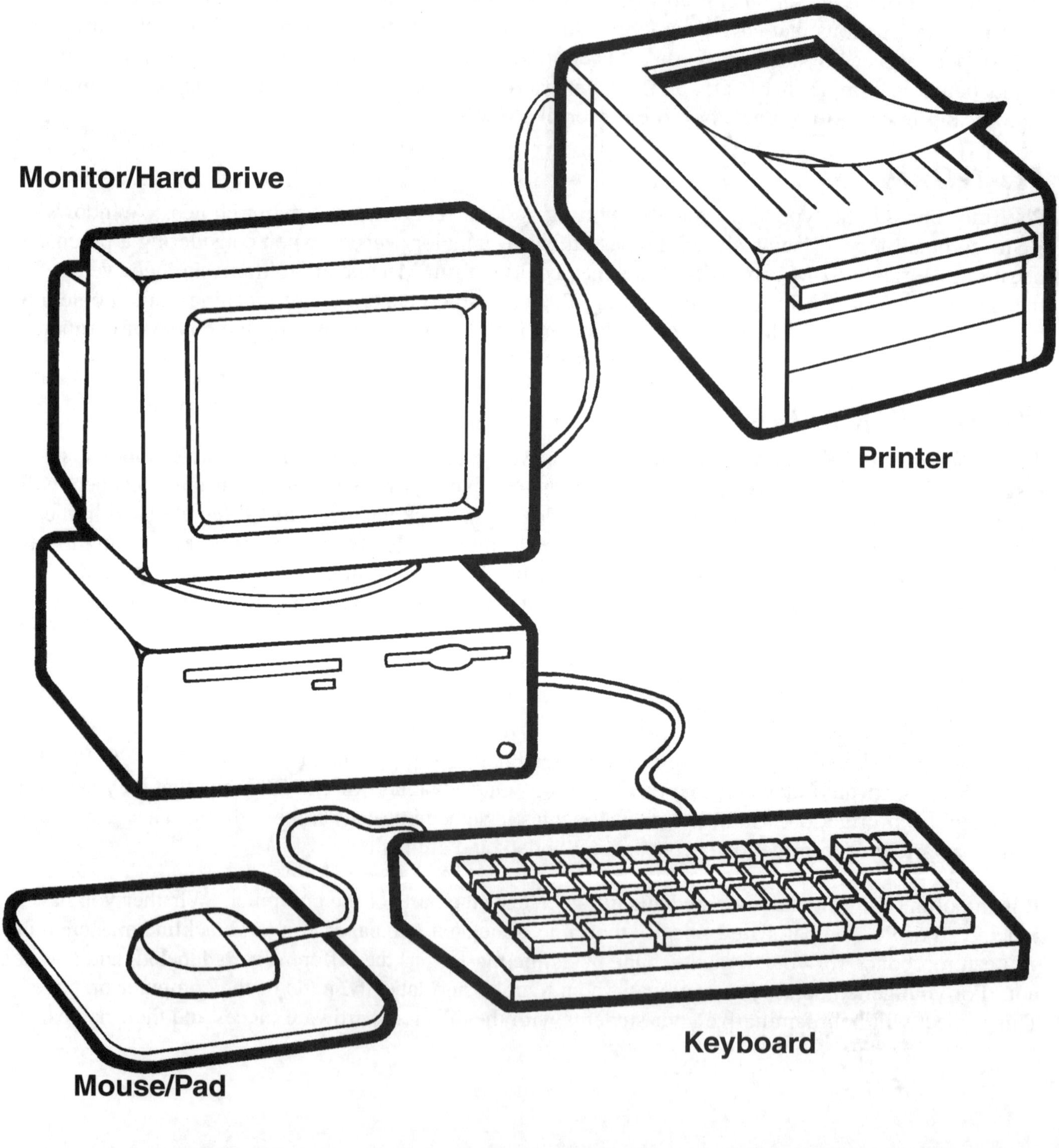

WHAT IS HARDWARE? *(cont.)*

HOW WILL YOU USE THE COMPUTER?

There are many ways to use the computer in your classroom. Below you will find different workable models.

- The Computer as a Teacher Productivity Resource
- The Computer as an Electronic Chalkboard or Large-Screen Projector
- The Computer Used to Access the Internet
- The Computer Used to Facilitate a Cooperative Learning Group
- The Computer as a Discussion Generator
- The Computer as a Skill Builder

As you are reading through this next section, think about the ways which you see yourself using the computer. The ultimate goal would be to incorporate a variety of the models discussed into your classroom. Although there are only brief descriptions provided, all of the models listed below will be discussed comprehensively throughout this book.

THE COMPUTER AS A TEACHER PRODUCTIVITY RESOURCE

Believe it or not, the computer sitting in your classroom can make your life much easier and simpler, although it may appear more complicated at first. Teachers can use the computer to compute grades, write parent newsletters or homework bulletins, create student portfolios, and communicate with colleagues. Often, teachers' lives can be revolutionized when they really begin to use the computer as a productivity tool. There are ideas, templates, and step-by-step directions for teachers to follow to use their one computer as a productivity tool in the next chapter. Also, on the CD-ROM enclosed with this book, you will find valuable templates for such projects as parent newsletters, homework bulletins, and electronic gradebooks.

THE COMPUTER AS AN ELECTRONIC CHALKBOARD OR LARGE-SCREEN PROJECTOR

Fortunately for educators and students, the computer programs produced today have graphics that are far superior to those which we can find quickly in the library or that we can produce ourselves without a lengthy time and talent involvement. An example of this is the fabulous animal pictures on the *Dorling Kindersley's Nature* CD-ROM which shows still pictures and movie clips. With careful selection of software, you can use large-screen presentations to greatly enhance the delivery of curriculum content.

There is really no reason that you cannot have a small group gather around your regular-sized computer monitor for a guided lesson. The software available today lends itself to adding depth to your lessons. Technology itself is just a tool to help you deliver the curriculum by aiding in the presentation of a lesson.

HOW WILL YOU USE THE COMPUTER? *(cont.)*

THE COMPUTER AS AN ELECTRONIC CHALKBOARD OR LARGE-SCREEN PROJECTOR *(cont.)*

In an ideal world, it would be wonderful to hook your computer to a TV or a large-screen projector. This may sound difficult or expensive, but actually it is not. Schools usually have a TV, and for a few hundred dollars, a teacher can project the computer easily onto the TV in order for students to better view it from a distance.

If you are fortunate enough to be able to project your computer screen, you can also make presentations for Back-to-School Night, highlighting your classroom and students' work. In addition, students can make presentations—using programs such as *Power Point* or *HyperStudio*—to present an entire project or create a visual aid for an oral report. There are more ideas and lesson plans for on-screen presentations in this section.

THE COMPUTER USED TO ACCESS THE INTERNET

The Internet is radically changing how we access information. Using the Internet allows the user to retrieve information, media, and even lesson plans from all over the world almost instantly. This book is full of Internet lesson plans and Web site addresses that will enhance your curriculum. But gathering information is merely one aspect of the power of the Internet—communication is the other. Once you have access to the Internet, you have access to all the users of the Internet—teachers sharing and collaborating with other teachers, students with other students, and students with experts in a variety of fields.

HOW WILL YOU USE THE COMPUTER? *(cont.)*

THE COMPUTER USED TO FACILITATE A COOPERATIVE LEARNING GROUP

A one-computer classroom can make good use of the technology by using it as a focal point in a cooperative learning strategy. Students are grouped and assigned projects to solve a particular problem. When the group meets, each student is given a role in the production of the project. One student is the scribe and takes notes on the group discussions about how they want to proceed with the project. One student heads the research team to decide what will be included in the project. One student is assigned to input the artwork and the other to input the text. The students can plan the entire project on notebook paper so they will be able to optimize their time on the computer.

These projects can be completely designed by you, the teacher, or you can use pre-made software designed to accomplish the same task. Tom Snyder's *Great Ocean Rescue* and *Rainforest Researchers* are simulation software titles; students are divided into cooperative learning groups and sent on a mission to solve a problem in the world.

This section will give you several ideas for cooperative learning projects which you can use in your classroom. Also, simulation software will be discussed thoroughly and software titles suggested.

HOW WILL YOU USE THE COMPUTER? *(cont.)*

THE COMPUTER AS A DISCUSSION GENERATOR

There are software packages available designed specifically to help you generate class discussion and decision making in the classroom with only one computer. Tom Snyder's software entitled *Choices, Choices* and *Decisions, Decisions* are examples of discussion-generating software. In *Decisions, Decisions: Immigration* the class becomes the president of the United States running for re-election. The primaries are approaching, and the class must decide their strategies to be nominated again in their party. A real-world crisis which the president must attend to interrupts their primary battles. This section will describe several discussion-generating software packages in detail.

THE COMPUTER AS A SKILL BUILDER

There are many fabulous pieces of software that have been created to reinforce a student's skills. Whether it is learning states and capitals, reviewing multiplication tables, or reinforcing phonics skills, there are hundreds of skill building pieces of software available. In this section, skill-building software will be discussed thoroughly with many specific titles of software suggested.

CLASSROOM MANAGEMENT

Having one computer or maybe even two computers in the classroom can be really exciting if managed properly. It is inevitable that you will hear "When is it my turn?" or "Mike got to work longer on the computer than I did." However, you can solve many of the inherent problems by implementing good management techniques.

The way you manage the computer in your classroom will primarily be based on the way you decide to use the computer. If the computer is used as a free-time activity where students play games, scheduling is not as much of an issue. See the traditional classroom model below. However, if you are integrating it into your teaching by including technology components in your units where students are responsible for producing technology projects, then you must provide larger blocks of equitable time on the computer. See the integrated classroom model below. The truth is that we all have unique teaching styles; therefore, we all will use technology in different ways. Hopefully, by the time you finish reading *The One-Computer Classroom,* you will be convinced of the many marvelous ways the computer can be used in the classroom.

Traditional Classroom Model

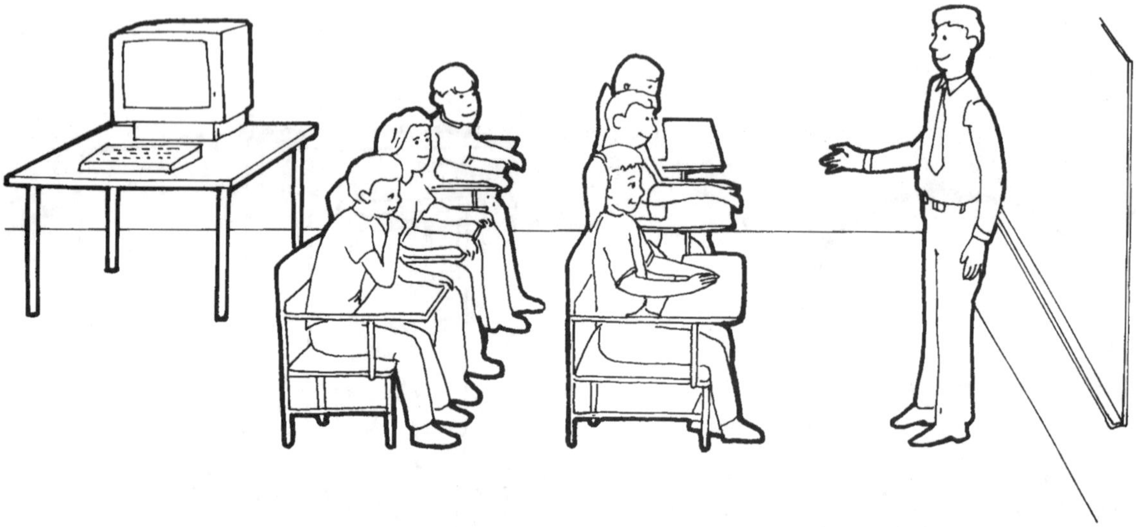

Integrated Classroom Model

PLACEMENT OF THE COMPUTER

Typically, all classrooms are too small and quite busy with lots of movement by both the teacher and students. This fact is of prime concern when deciding on computer placement in the classroom. Before setting up your classroom for the addition of your computer, it is important to ask yourself this question—what will I primarily use the computer for? The answer to this question will greatly determine the "home base" where your computer will be located most of the time. Review pages 8–10 to decide how you will be using your computer.

If you will mostly be using the classroom computer as a presentation and cooperative learning tool for your lessons, then you will want to set up your classroom similar to the diagram found on page 14. This type of setup will also be beneficial for student presentations.

If the fundamental use for the classroom computer is more of a workstation for independent work, long-term projects, or skill building, then you will want to set up your classroom similar to the diagram found on page 15. Try to place an extra table near the computer station so cooperative learning groups will have a place to meet and collaborate.

Finally, if you envision your computer primarily being used by you, the teacher, for recordkeeping, correspondence, portfolio management, and overall personal assistance to manage your day, follow the diagram found on page 16.

Ideally, it would be a good idea to put the computer on a cart with wheels or a table with wheels. Most educators in one-computer classrooms find the computer is used for a variety of purposes and ends up being moved around quite often.

PLACEMENT OF THE COMPUTER *(cont.)*

DIAGRAM 1

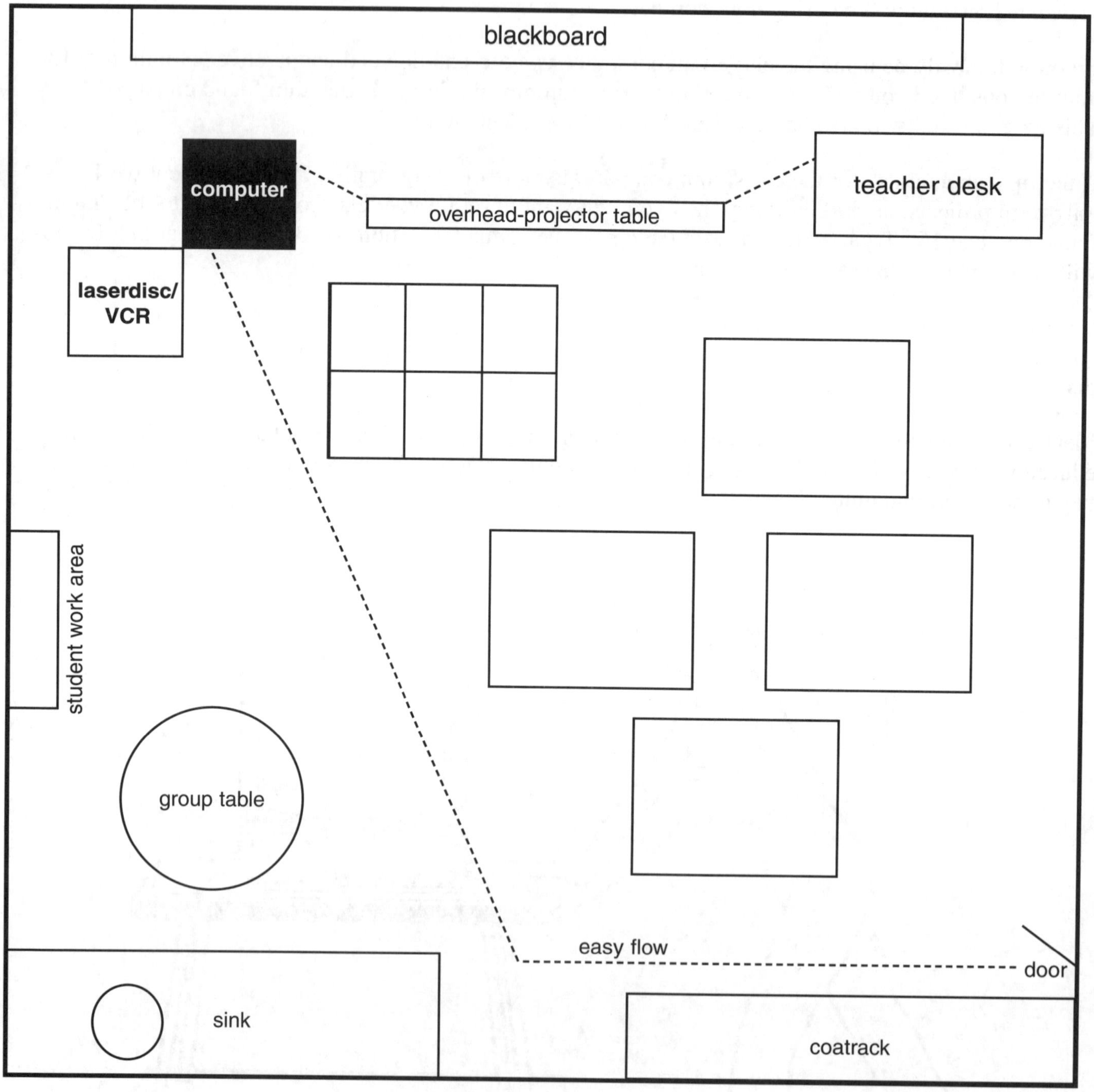

PLACEMENT OF THE COMPUTER *(cont.)*

DIAGRAM 2

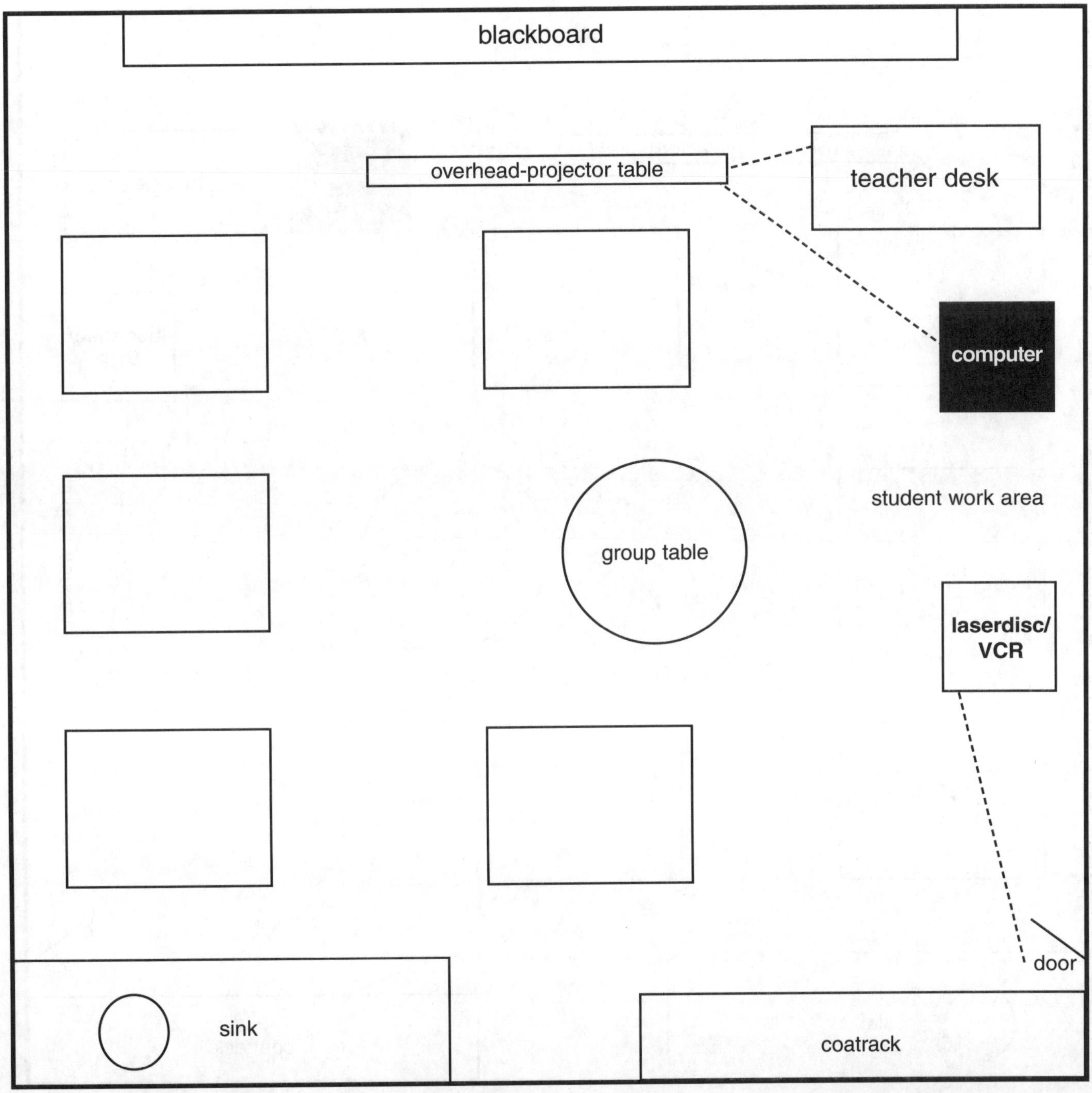

PLACEMENT OF THE COMPUTER *(cont.)*

DIAGRAM 3

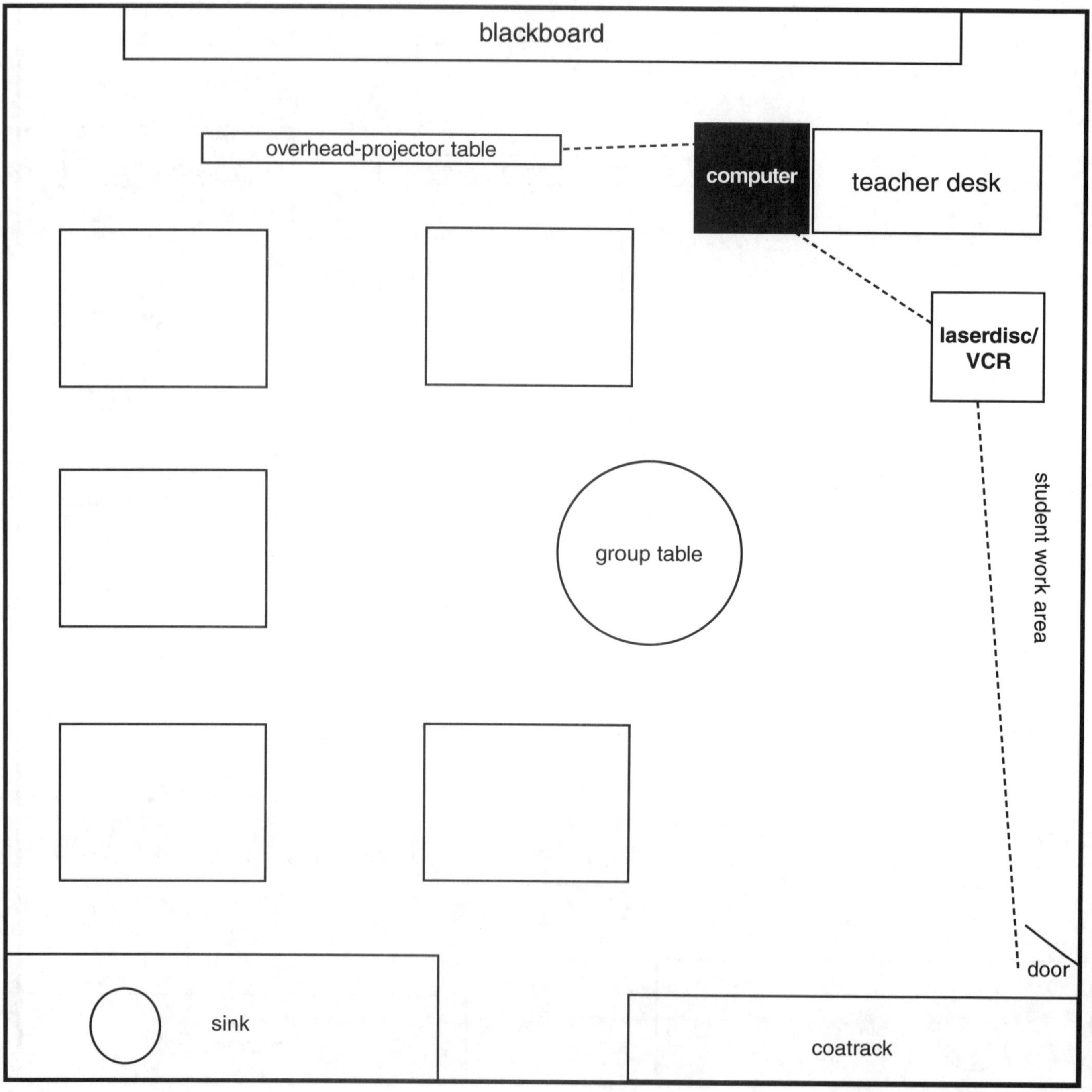

SCHEDULING

SCHEDULING TIME ON THE COMPUTER

If you are using the computer in a situation where it stands alone and is to be used by as many students as possible during the week, you will need to decide on a schedule for use. Depending on your preferences, you might want to schedule blocks of time where students are assigned to the computer in pairs or small groups. Alternatively, you might prefer the computer to be in use all day with students working in pairs or independently for a shorter length of time. In either case you will need to draw up a schedule and post it in plain sight.

SCHEDULING EXAMPLE

When assigning students to a block of time, you can group them in mixed ability groups, and they can choose a name or you give them a color-code (blue group, yellow group, etc.). For example, if the purple group is on the computer during the math block, the four to five students in the group may work on the computer during that time. During each week or each unit, every group should have computer time during every block. For some units, the technology component may be a group activity so all students in the group are contributing. When you assign an individual activity, students take turns at the computer based on who is prepared and ready for the computer activity. This method may sound like a scheduling nightmare, but it is surprising how easily students are able to adjust once a routine is set.

MIXED ABILITY GROUPS

Blue Group	Yellow Group	Red Group	Purple Group	Green Group
BOB	AUSTIN	DARYL	RENEE	JOHN
DAWN	GEORGE	DIANE	KIMBERLY	JILL
KYLE	MIKE	BILL	JASON	ERIN
BARBARA	BYRON	PAMELA	GARY	DOREEN
MANUEL	JOE	CAROL	JUAN	TERESA

SCHEDULING *(cont.)*

To keep track of whose group is scheduled for computer time during the day, use a paper clip to hang a string from the ceiling over the computer. At each block changeover, hang the coordinating color of construction paper over the technology center. This signals the group that at some point during the small-group activities, they may work on the computer.

Hint: Make one of your daily helpers the technology manager. This person will be in charge of changing the group assignment clip at the computer to alert the group to their computer time.

Sample Schedule:

Block	Monday	Tuesday	Wednesday	Thursday	Friday
Math	Purple	Blue	Red	Yellow	Green
Writer's Workshop	Blue	Red	Yellow	Green	Purple
Thematic Unit	Green	Yellow	Blue	Purple	Red
Language Arts	Yellow	Green	Purple	Red	Blue

EQUITY

Making sure all your students have the opportunity to work on the computer can be very difficult. There are ways to make it easier to manage for you and your students. Choose a visual way to display who has and has not been to the computer. Regardless of how you schedule student time on the computer, this is a successful way to make sure one person is not monopolizing the computer.

The methods on this page and page 19 allow you, the teacher, and the students to do a quick scan to see who has had a recent turn on the computer and who still needs the opportunity.

Craft Sticks

Materials: marker, craft stick for every student, two jars/cups

Put each student's name on a craft stick. Label one jar "not yet" and one jar "been there." At the beginning of the week or unit, all students start out in the "not yet" jar. Once they have had turns on the computer, they must put their craft sticks in the "been there" jar. This does not mean they cannot use a computer a second time. Whenever the computer is available, it is fair game. However, it does mean that students in the "not yet" jar can bump a student off the computer by taking their craft sticks from the "not yet" jar. You never want your computer to gather dust when it can be productive; however, you do need to allow opportunity for all students.

SCHEDULING *(cont.)*

Clothespins

Materials: poster board (one piece), one clothespin for each student.

Put each student's name on a clothespin. Draw a line down the middle of the poster board. The left side is reserved for students who have not been to the computer; the right side is for those who have been. Once they have had a turn on the computer, they move their clothespins to the other side. Perhaps on this side you could list alternative independent activities once each student has worked on a computer (writer's workshop, reading corner, research, puzzle center, etc.).

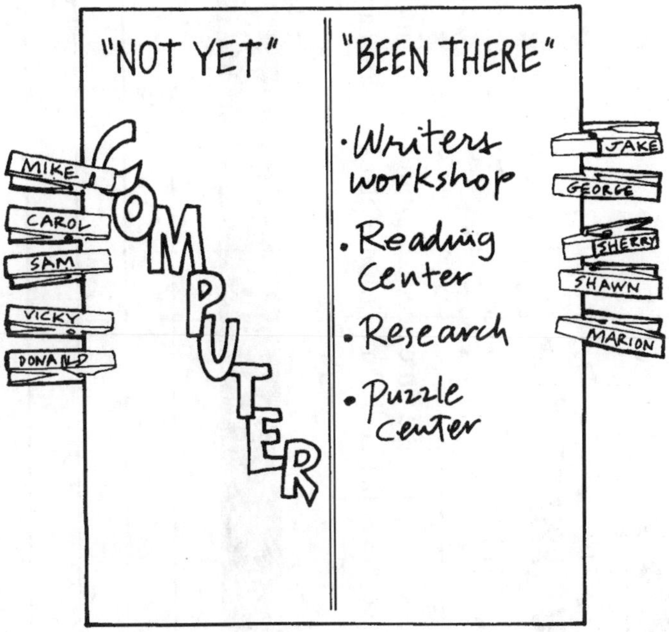

SIGN-UP SHEET

You may want to use some blocks of time during your day as priority-based computer time. To use this time, students must sign up to work on a particular project and justify why they need the computer time. For example, if a student's project crashes or if a student is absent, that student may need extra computer time, as compared to a student who just wants to add some snazzy animation or play a problem-solving game for fun. You can decide the order and the amount of time that each student will have to work on a computer. This block of time could be first thing in the morning, during silent reading time, or some other consistent block of time during the day. Keep a sign-up sheet for each week on a clipboard near the technology center. There is a sign-up sheet on page 20, or make your own.

CLASSROOM MEETING

Hold a class meeting to get scheduling suggestions from your students. Share some different scheduling possibilities with them and ask them to share their thoughts and ideas. You will be amazed at some of the wonderful ideas students have to offer. Also, the majority of students often find it easier to follow rules and schedules that they have had a part in creating.

You may find that none of these methods alone will solve all of your scheduling problems. Try a combination of these methods. Maybe you can create your own scheduling variation. Because your classroom is unique, your scheduling needs are, as well. Just do not let your computer sit idle.

SCHEDULING *(cont.)*

COMPUTER SIGN-UP SHEET

WEEK OF ________________

Students: Be sure to fill in your name, project, reason you need to work on it, and the time needed to finish it. If any of these columns are left blank, your request will not be considered. Leave the Scheduled Time column blank so you can be assigned a time.

Student Name	Project	Reason	Time Needed	Scheduled Time

WHAT SHOULD I HAVE ALONG WITH THE COMPUTER?

It is recommended that students have their own disks with their names on them as soon as they know how to save their work. Place these disks in a plastic disk container next to the computer for ready access. Many of the disks today are sold preformatted as either Mac or IBM compatible, and are ready for use out of the box. Name each disk with the student's name and the year. This way, when students put the disks in the computer to save their work, they see their names on the screen and know it is OK to save. At the end of the quarter or semester, disks containing a portfolio of their computer work can be sent home. Remember that disks easily fail; it is always a good idea to have a backup either as a copy on another disk, on the hard drive, or on a school network. If your school has a network, you may be able to create individual student folders where work can be saved on the network.

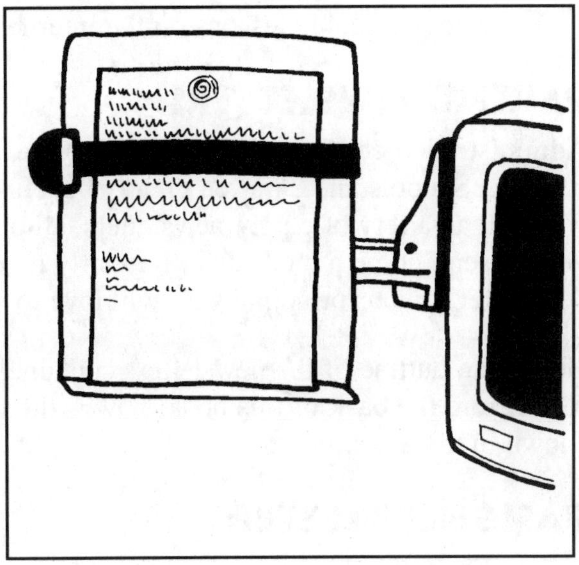

Equip your computer with an attachment that has a large clip to hold work the students are inputting. These clips are very handy and quite inexpensive. You could find this type of computer clip at any computer store or office supply store.

Hopefully, you have a printer next to your computer or access to one. Students will love to see their work in printed form, and it really looks attractive displayed around the room. If you are really lucky, you may have a color printer. Color printers have significantly come down in price and will last a long time if used conservatively. If you decide to buy a color printer, Hewlett Packard makes a fine product for both the Mac and the PC.

HELPFUL TIP

Place a red cup and a blue cup next to the computer monitor. The red cup should be placed on the top of the monitor when help is needed. The blue cup should be placed on the top of the monitor when something cool has been done on the computer. Both of these methods will prevent students from constantly disturbing the class and allow you as the teacher to quickly notice good progress on the computer.

TEACHER TOOLS

I have the privilege of doing a lot of technology training with teachers all across the country. The complaint I hear most often from teachers is "I don't have enough time!" I have found that when teachers learned to use the computer proficiently, they began to actually save themselves time.

The next several pages will be devoted to making your life easier and more efficient as a teacher. There will be several corresponding templates that you can find on the CD-ROM enclosed with this book. We will discuss ways to increase your teacher productivity in areas such as the following:

- creating parent newsletters and homework bulletins
- making an electronic grade book for student assessment
- creating student portfolios
- locating valuable lessons on the Internet.

PARENT NEWSLETTERS

Administration continues to impress upon teachers the need to communicate often and effectively to parents. Schools and children greatly benefit from parents being informed. On the next few pages, you will find a variety of parent newsletters, all of which have been created on the computer. Make it your goal to send home a monthly or quarterly parent newsletter. Don't forget to give a copy of the newsletter to your principal who will love to see how technology is transforming your classroom.

Here is an outline of the newsletters contained on the following pages. If you haven't opened your CD-ROM from the back of this book, now is the time. You will find templates for all of the newsletters shown in this book on the CD-ROM.

BASIC NEWSLETTER

p. 23 Example of a basic newsletter to parents done in *Claris Works*

p. 24 Blank template of this basic newsletter on the CD-ROM

INTERMEDIATE NEWSLETTER

p. 25 Example of a monthly or quarterly parent newsletter done in *Claris Works*

p. 26 Blank template of the intermediate newsletter on the CD-ROM

TEACHER TOOLS *(cont.)*

This is an example of a basic newsletter to parents—done in *ClarisWorks*.

November 1

Dear Parents,

It has been a busy fall, and I wanted to personally thank each parent who helped us get off to a great start this year. Your children are eager to learn and a real pleasure to teach.

I wanted to take a moment to highlight a few units we are studying this month. We have started two digit multiplication in math. Any reinforcement of the multiplication tables at home would be very helpful. For our reading unit, we have begun to read *Julie of the Wolves* by Scott O'Dell. We will be reading about two chapters a week. We have just finished studying the Southern states in Social Studies and will be starting the Midwest states next week. Don't forget your child has a States and Capitals quiz at the end of studying each region. Lastly, we are learning about plants in science and will be growing our own bean plants soon. As you can see, your students are busy in Mrs. Harrison's 4th grade class!

We will be starting a canned food drive next week with the other 4th grade classes. We are hoping that each child can bring 2-3 canned foods by November 15. We will be making baskets that will be distributed to needy families. Thanks for your help!

Finally, I want to thank you for a great turn-out for Parent-Teacher Conferences. You are a big part of your child's success.

Sincerely,

Mrs. Harrison

TEACHER TOOLS *(cont.)*

This is the blank template of the basic newsletter found on the CD-ROM.

Type Date

Dear Parents,

Type your initial greeting to parents. Consider thanking parents for something they did recently.

Highlight what you are studying in class. Include past accomplishments and upcoming projects.

Discuss important dates for parents to remember like the school carnival or Open House Night.

Closing. Try to think of a "warm fuzzy" to end the letter.

Sincerely,

Your name.

TEACHER TOOLS *(cont.)*

This is an example of a monthly or quarterly parent newsletter done in *ClarisWorks*.

January Newsletter for Mr. Phillip's Class

Frogs, Frogs, and More Frogs

We have been studying frogs in science class. We explored an excellent CD-ROM called *Nature* by Dorling Kindersley. Via the CD-ROM we saw a real frog dissection! We studied about a frog's habitat and created our own in a fish tank. We will be getting two frogs to live in our tank next week.

Helping the Needy

Thanks to all of you who helped make the holidays special for families in need. Your children brought over 45 gently used items items to class. We then boxed and wrapped this gifts. We created short holiday poems for each family. Thanks to you, we were able to help over 10 families in need last December! We have wonderful kids at Highland Middle School!

Mark Your Calendars!

Mark your calendars for the upcoming events at Highland Middle School.

Book Reports Due:	Friday, January 22
Spelling Bee:	Tuesday, February 2 at 10:00
Valentine Dance:	Friday, February 12 at 7:00 pm
Science Fair:	February 21-26
Spring Break:	March 15-19

TEACHER TOOLS *(cont.)*

This is an example of a monthly or quarterly parent newsletter done in *Claris Works*.

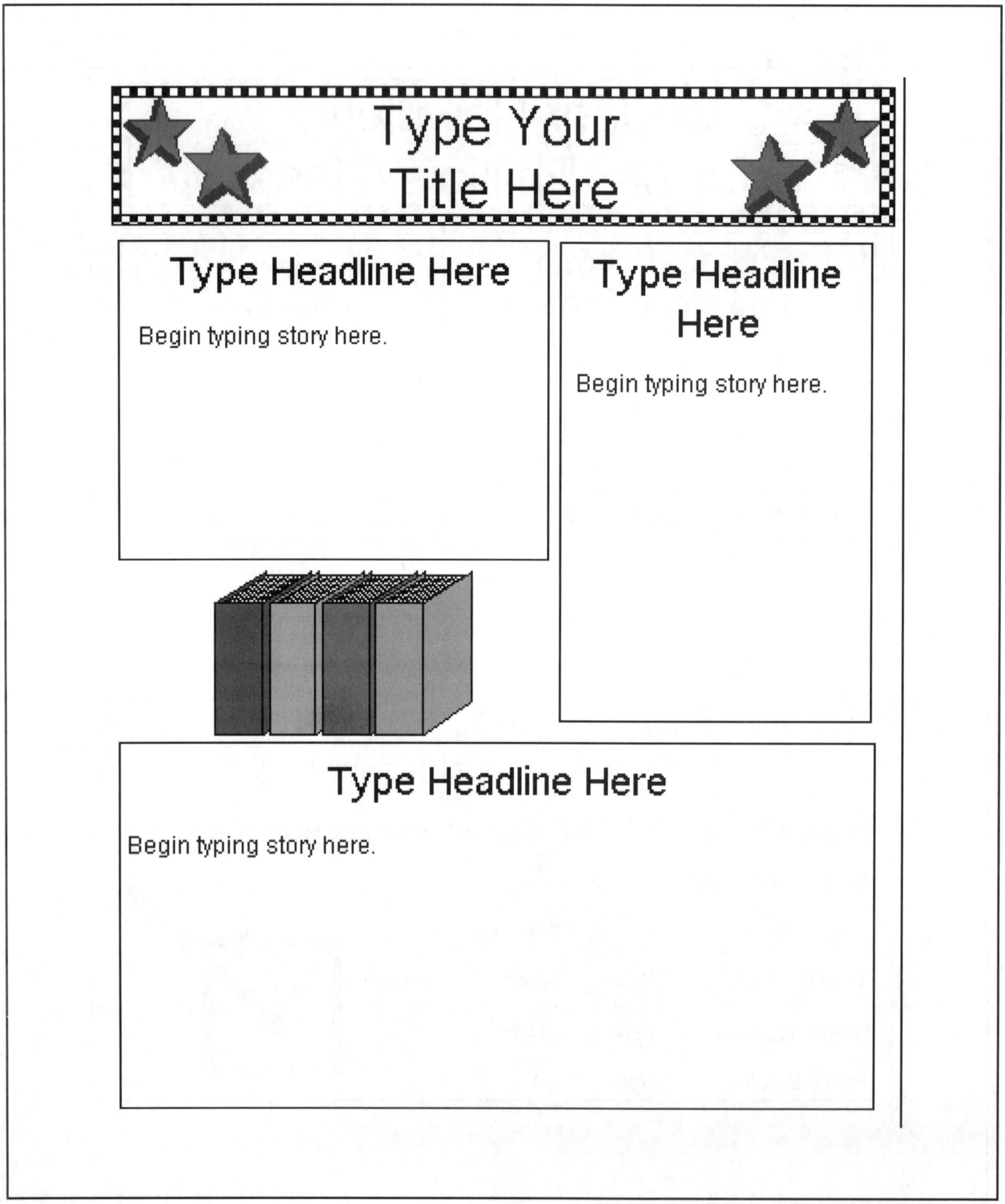

Type Your Title Here

Type Headline Here

Begin typing story here.

Type Headline Here

Begin typing story here.

Type Headline Here

Begin typing story here.

TEACHER TOOLS *(cont.)*

HOMEWORK BULLETINS

Homework bulletins are a favorite for students and parents. These bulletins can be as simple as a list of the homework and upcoming activities, or you may want to add more information such as highlighting student accomplishments or adding a thought for the week. I have completely converted teachers to technology by helping them make homework bulletins. You will be surprised how many parents will compliment you on your homework bulletins.

You will find an example of a homework bulletin and template on pages 28–29. A copy of the template is also found on the CD-ROM.

You can find cute clip art in a variety of places. Often the program itself will have clip art which is the case in *Microsoft Word* and *ClarisWorks*. You may want to use a paint program such as *Kid Pix* to create your homework bulletin and decorate it with the stamps. There are also many CD-ROMs available that contain clip art. These CD-ROMs can be rather inexpensive ($10.00), but more elaborate clip art galleries will run fifty or more dollars. If you do buy a clip art CD-ROM, make sure you read the box to find out if it is for a Mac or PC. Most clip art galleries are not in hybrid format.

TEACHER TOOLS *(cont.)*

Example of homework bulletin done in Claris Works. Homework Bulletin.

Mrs. Keating's Homework Bulletin

Date: Sept. 6-10 Theme: Transportation

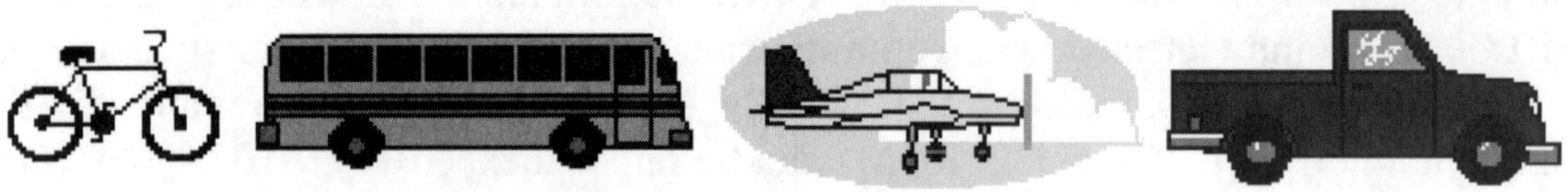

MONDAY:	**Do Math pg. 9 Find 2 examples of transportation at your house.**
TUESDAY:	**Read 10 minutes to a parent. Write 7 examples of transportation.**
WEDNESDAY:	**Do Math pg. 11 Review addition flash cards.**
THURSDAY:	**Spelling Test over List #3. Write a short story about our visit with the fireman today.**
FRIDAY:	**Read 10 minutes to a parent.**
OTHER INFO:	**Mr. Thomas the fireman will be bringing his big tanker to school on Wednesday. Parents, feel free to join us at 10:00 for this exciting event!**

TEACHER TOOLS *(cont.)*

Blank template of the homework bulletin on the CD-ROM Homework Bulletin Template

Homework Bulletin

Date: Theme:

MONDAY:	**Start typing here.**
TUESDAY:	**Start typing here.**
WEDNESDAY:	**Start typing here.**
THURSDAY:	**Start typing here.**
FRIDAY:	**Start typing here.**
OTHER INFO:	**Start typing here.**

STUDENT ASSESSMENT—ELECTRONIC GRADE BOOKS

For a teacher, student assessment can be very time consuming and tedious. One of the computer's original uses was to calculate numbers. In the blink of an eye, the computer can compute thousands of numbers. Wouldn't this help you tremendously when it is time to average grades? With a little extra preliminary work, teachers can create an incredible electronic grade book which can be used year after year.

Let's first take a look at a basic spreadsheet. Look at Figure 1. Notice there are many empty boxes (called cells) with A, B, C across the top and 1, 2 ,3 going down.

Figure 1

	A	B	C	D	E	F	G
1							
2							
3							
4							
5							
6							
7							
8							
9							

In Figure 2, you can see names, data, and formulas have been entered in these cells. Notice that the far right column labeled "I" has the students' averages. There is a formula in this cell which tells the computer to average all of the scores.

Figure 2

	A	B	C	D	E	F	G	H	I
1		HW 1	Quiz 1	HW 2	Quiz 2	HW 3	HW 4		Final AVG
3	Amy	65	80	100	88	85	80		83
4	Brian	80	85	100	78	75	90		85
5	Heather	85	90	80	88	85	90		86
6	Jacob	84	90	90	82	85	100		89
7	Karen	88	95	90	88	95	90		91
8	Mary	75	70	80	78	70	85		76
9	Michael	87	80	90	94	85	100		89
10	Scott	78	75	90	78	80	90		82
11	Susan	91	85	95	94	85	90		90

STUDENT ASSESSMENT—ELECTRONIC GRADE BOOKS *(cont.)*

STEPS TO MAKE YOU OWN ELECTRONIC GRADE BOOK

- Open a spreadsheet program such as *Microsoft Excel* or the spreadsheet feature in *ClarisWorks*. A blank spreadsheet form will appear.
- Click in cell A3 and begin to type your class roster. Type only one item in each box.
- In the first row across, type the categories you want, such as HW 1, Test 1, etc. Look at Figure 2 on page 30.
- Now enter the students' scores.

	A	B	C	D	E
1		HW 1	HW 2	HW 2	AVG
3	Amy	65	80	100	
4	Brian	80	85	100	
5	Heather	85	90	80	
6	Jacob	84	90	90	
7	Karen	88	95	90	

- Next, you will need to make a formula to average the scores. In order to average, you will need to tell the computer to add all of the scores and divide by the number of scores. To do this, you will click on the first student's final average cell. Then you will type a formula similar to this, depending on how many scores you have: =AVERAGE(B3:D3).
- Once you have typed this formula, then press enter or return. The student's final average should appear. Double-check it with a calculator. If the average is correct, copy this formula all the way down the average column.

HELPFUL TIP

All formulas entered on a spreadsheet begin with the equals sign. You will find the above grade book spreadsheet on the CD-ROM, but the scores and names will be blank.

STUDENT ASSESSMENT—ELECTRONIC GRADE BOOKS *(cont.)*

ADVANCED GRADE BOOK SPREADSHEETS

Below you find an example of a more complicated grade book spreadsheet. It still follows the basic rules; however, more detailed information has been added. Notice the class averages are at the bottom. The final average has been weighted; tests are weighted twice as much as homework assignments.

	A	B	C	D	E	F	G	H	I	J
1	Last	First	Test 1	Test 2	**T. Avg**	HW 1	HW2	**HW Avg**		**Final AVG**
3	Allen	Valerie	89	92	91	80	85	83		88
4	Alvarez	Juan	78	96	87	70	95	83		86
5	Benson	Sarah	86	82	84	90	75	83		84
6	Brighten	Zack	85	76	81	100	70	85		82
7	Brown	Amy	98	65	82	50	65	58		74
8	Houston	William	65	84	75	60	75	68		72
9	Jackson	Rob	89	67	78	90	70	80		79
10	Koller	Holly	77	82	80	70	80	75		78
11	Larson	Taylor	92	89	91	80	85	83		88
12	Mitts	Julie	96	86	91	70	95	83		88
13	Morrison	Nathan	82	70	76	80	85	83		78
14	Norrion	Cindy	76	98	87	80	80	80		85
15	O'Sullivan	Ben	65	85	75	90	70	80		77
16	Peterson	Mike	84	98	91	100	95	98		93
17	Savage	Laura	67	65	66	70	60	65		66
18	Smith	Shelly	82	89	86	80	65	73		81
19	Sutton	Brittany	89	77	83	70	70	70		79
20	Tollen	Chuck	86	92	89	90	85	88		89
21	Volden	Mark	70	96	83	70	65	68		78
22	Young	Paul	98	82	90	80	60	70		83
23										
24	**Class Avg**		83	84	83	79	77	78		81

STUDENT ASSESSMENT—ELECTRONIC GRADE BOOKS *(cont.)*

COMMERCIAL GRADE BOOK PROGRAMS

There are several commercial pieces of software which will compute grades available to teachers. Some of these programs can be rather simple and inexpensive while other programs are incredibly comprehensive and costly. One recommended grade book program is called *Grade Machine Deluxe* by Misty City Software. You can buy this program through Tom Snyder Productions at 1-800-342-0236, and the cost is $70.00. With some dedicated grade book programs, you can create customized printouts, averages, distributions, and graphs—all at the press of a key.

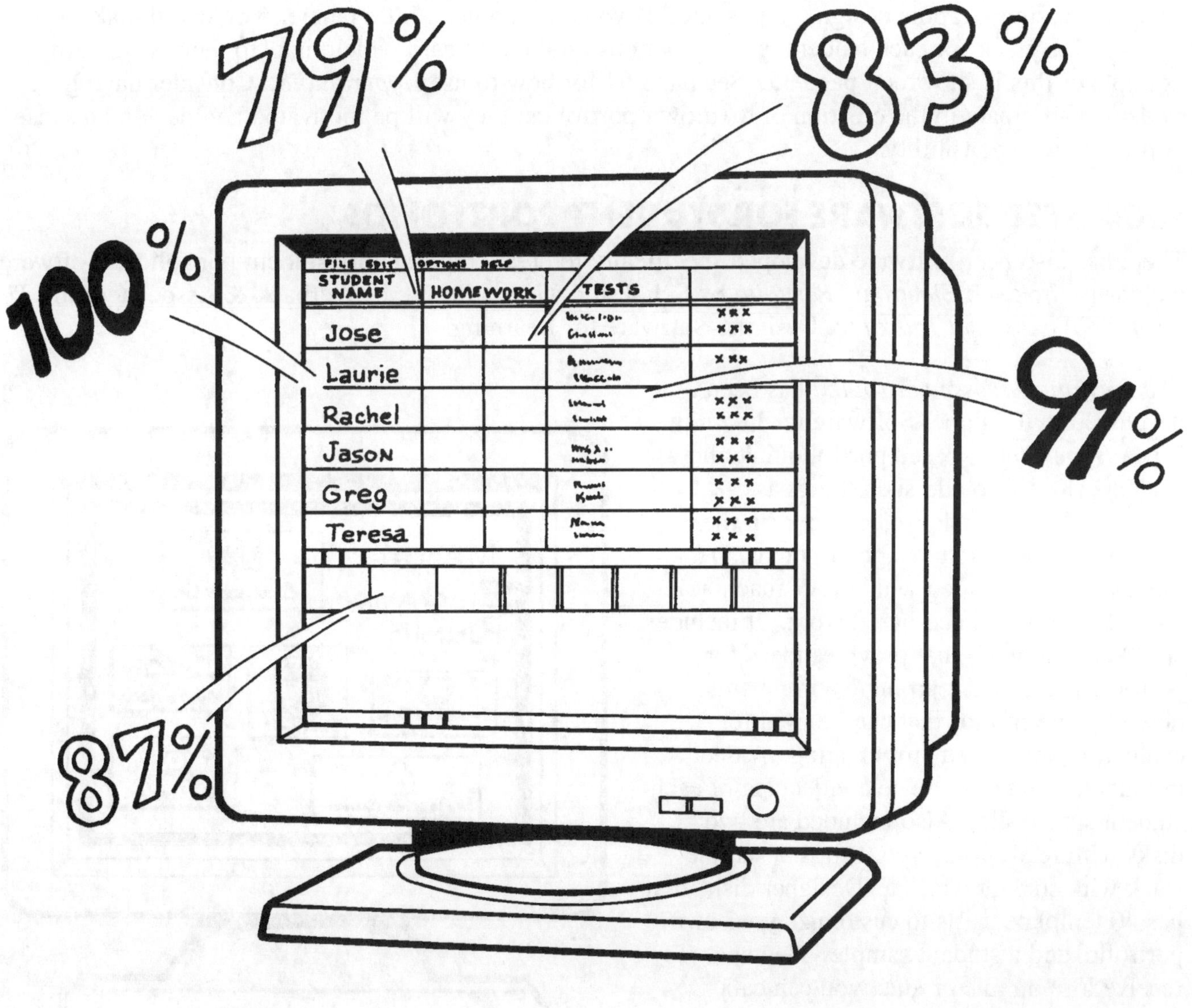

STUDENT ASSESSMENT—STUDENT PORTFOLIOS

CREATING STUDENT PORTFOLIOS

Portfolios are a compelling and concrete way to display student progress over time and are rapidly becoming an integral part of the classroom. Simply stated, a portfolio is a collection of student work showing where the student started, the progress the student has made, and a sense of what the student is capable of doing.

Electronic portfolios are powerful tools which transform the traditional paper portfolios into exciting multimedia presentations while solving the storage problem at the same time. One of the main drawbacks to paper-based portfolio management is the storage and fragility of the actual folder. An electronic portfolio could be as simple as saving all of a child's work on a separate disk. Then at the end of the semester or year, the teacher and students could organize the work in separate folders such as word processing, graphic design, graphs, etc. If you want to get a little fancier, you could make a *HyperStudio* stack for each student, putting buttons on the first card which links to their work. An example of this is shown on page 35. See page 57 for how to use *HyperStudio.* Consider having students participate in the creation of their own portfolios; they will be motivated and develop a sense of pride and responsibility.

SUGGESTED SOFTWARE FOR STUDENT PORTFOLIOS

There has also been software developed specifically to create high-quality student portfolios. Software includes *Scholastic Electronic Portfolio* by Scholastic, *Grady Profile* by Aurback & Associates, and *The Portfolio Assessment Toolkit* by Designer Software for Learning.

The Portfolio Assessment Toolkit has been developed by Designer Software for Learning. It is a *HyperStudio*-based portfolio that allows students (K–12) to add such things as activities, books read, project work (in the form of scanned pictures, photographs, QT movies, and live video with an AV machine) and other performance-based work. It includes an 80-page manual that provides ideas for performance-based learning environments, how-to-write rubrics that can be used for evaluation, and details for creating a video production center to create a videotape of each student's portfolio. Also included are two disks with ready-to-use portfolios, a sample stack with student work, a "Designer disk" that has 40 template cards to customize your own portfolio, and a student sample videotape. To receive info on this product you can call Designer Software at (303) 693-1212.

STUDENT ASSESSMENT—STUDENT PORTFOLIOS *(cont.)*

BASIC STUDENT PORTFOLIO DONE IN HYPERSTUDIO

Below you will find an example of a basic portfolio done in *HyperStudio*. You will find this same template on the CD-ROM.

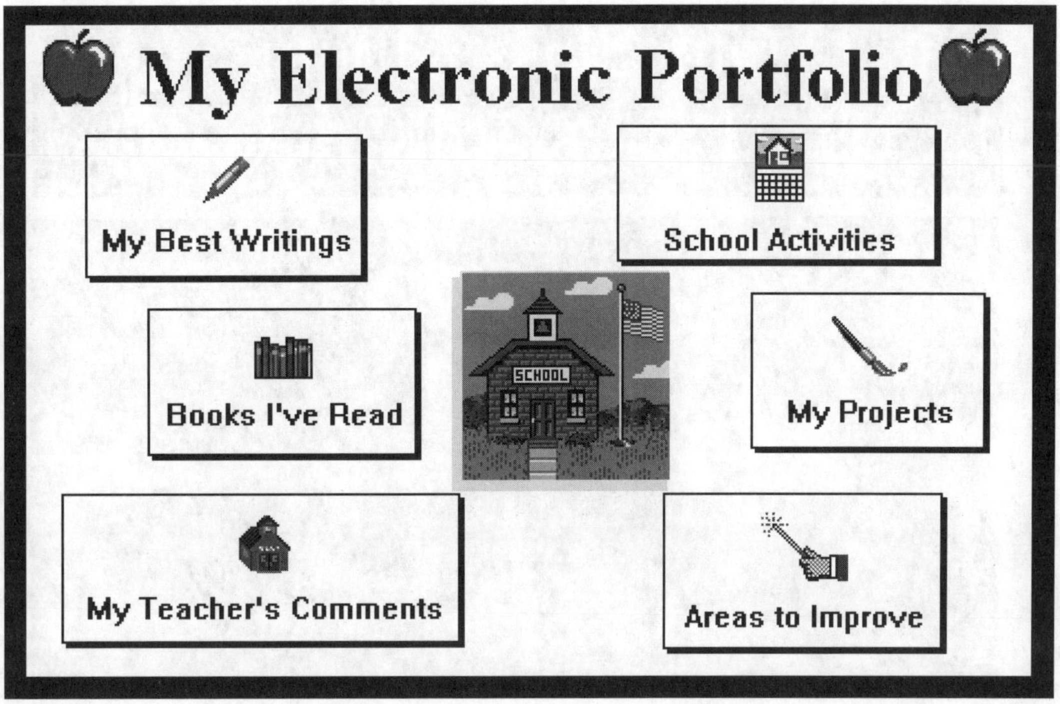

STUDENT ASSESSMENT—STUDENT PORTFOLIOS *(cont.)*

ADVANCED STUDENT PORTFOLIO DONE IN HYPERSTUDIO

Below you will find an example of a advanced portfolio done in *HyperStudio*. You will find this same template on the CD-ROM.

FINDING LESSON PLANS ON THE INTERNET

There are many fabulous Web sites which have tried-and-true lesson plans from teachers in the field. Why should you reinvent the wheel if someone already has! At one time, I taught a comprehensive unit on oceans to my fourth graders. Year after year I would try to create new projects for the ocean unit. Little did I know that on the Internet, there were hundreds of lesson plans which teachers have created just on oceans!

Throughout the following pages, several Web sites that can be used as a teacher tool will be highlighted. If you have been on the Internet before, then you will have no problem finding these Web sites. If you are a beginner, then skip to page 62 to gain an overview of the Internet and how to use it.

Here is a list of five excellent Web sites which will provide you thousands of lessons plans on a variety of topics and age levels.

Name:

GEM The Gateway to Educational Materials

URL:

http://www.thegateway.org

Description of Site:

The Gateway provides the key to one-stop, any-stop access to high-quality Internet lesson plans, curriculum units, and other education resources. Conduct full-text, subject, keyword, or title searches, and then select the desired grade or education level and submit the search. Retrieved records will link directly to the Internet resources they describe—it's that easy! The Gateway currently contains 1,550 education resources.

FINDING LESSON PLANS ON THE INTERNET *(cont.)*

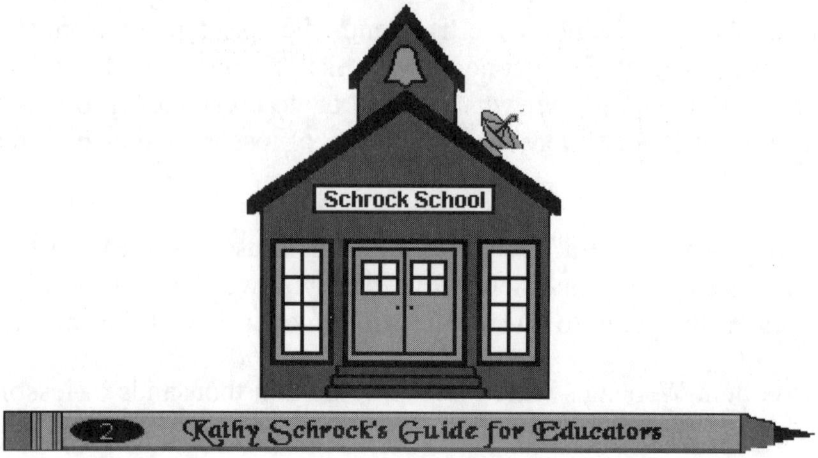

Name:
Kathy Schrock's Guide for Educators

URL:
http://discoveryschool.com/schrockguide/

Description of Site:
Kathy Schrock's Guide for Educators is a classified list of sites on the Internet found to be useful for enhancing curriculum and teacher professional growth. This site is organized by topic and updated daily to keep up with the tremendous number of new World Wide Web sites.

Busy Teachers' WebSite K-12

Name:
Busy Teachers' Web Site K–12

URL:
http://www.ceismc.gatech.edu/busyt

Description of Site:
Busy Teachers' Web Site provides teachers with direct source materials, lesson plans/classroom activities with a minimum of site-to-site linking, and an enjoyable and rewarding experience for the teacher who is learning to use the Internet. At this Web site, you will many topics pertinent to the classroom.

FINDING LESSON PLANS ON THE INTERNET *(cont.)*

Name:
Teach Net

URL:
http://www.teachnet.com

Description of Site:
Teach Net was started in August 1995 by the husband/wife team of Lee Shiney (graphic designer and writer) and Lajean Shiney (4th–5th grade teacher at Lawrence Elementary School, USD 259, Wichita, Kansas. After being introduced to the Internet, they immediately saw the potential for this technology as a communications vehicle for educators. Since then, Teach Net has grown to the size you see, including over 6,000 subscribers to the e-mail newsletter, and over 1,000 regular users of the postings mailing list.

Name:
AskERIC Lesson Plans

URL:
http://ericir.syr.edu/Virtual/Lessons

Description of Site:
The Educational Resources Information Center (ERIC) is a federally funded national information system which began in 1992 as a project of the ERIC Clearinghouse on Information & Technology at Syracuse University. The lesson plan site is one of the most comprehensive on the Internet. It contains lessons for all subjects and all grade levels.

CONNECTING YOUR COMPUTER TO ANOTHER DISPLAY

THE COMPUTER AS AN ELECTRONIC CHALKBOARD

Think about how you use your chalkboard in your classroom right now. Probably you present information, illustrate ideas, manage your classroom, and do a host of other things. Now let's imagine a chalkboard on which you could present material larger and in color, archive presentations easily for future lessons, show real pictures or video footage. Believe it or not, this can be done easily and not too expensively by hooking your computer to a projection device such as a television, LCD panel, or large-screen projector. Once you hook up your computer to one of the projection devices, you have a great tool to make stimulating presentations to your class! You can easily save these presentations and use them from class to class or year to year.

The next few pages will discuss the three most popular projection devices: a television, LCD panel, and a large-screen projector.

CONNECTING YOUR OLDER COMPUTER TO A TELEVISION

Older computers such as Apple II, Laser, Radio Shack, and Commodore computers popular in the 1980s used regular video line signals. Because of this, these computers are very easy to display on a large-screen television. You simply split the video line coming out of the back of the computer by attaching a Y cable (available for under seven dollars at any electronics store). This allows the computer to be seen at both its monitor and on the television. See the diagram below for connecting.

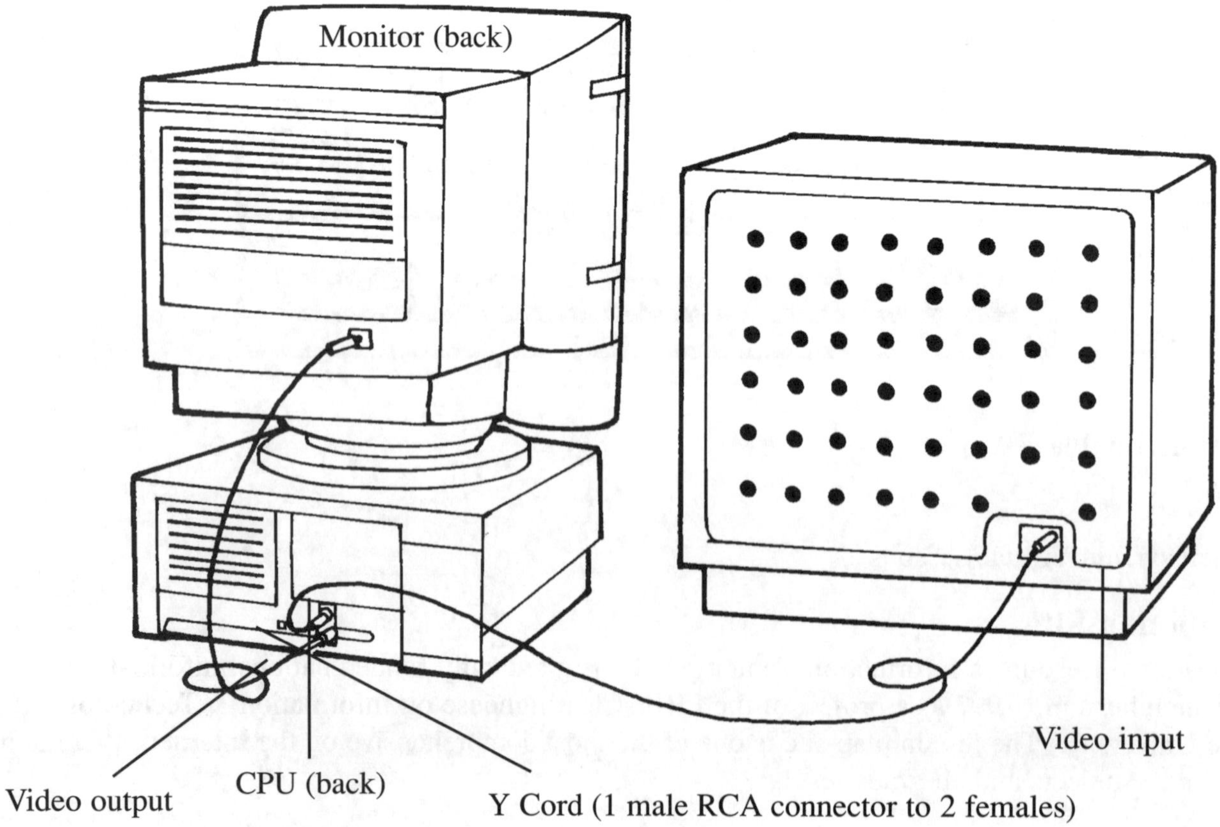

CONNECTING YOUR COMPUTER TO ANOTHER DISPLAY *(cont.)*

CONNECTING YOUR OLDER COMPUTER TO A TELEVISION *(cont.)*

If your television does not have a video line input or you wish to videotape what is on the computer, use the diagram below. If you do not have a VCR or a TV that has video line input or S video input, you will need to purchase an RF converter from an electronics store.

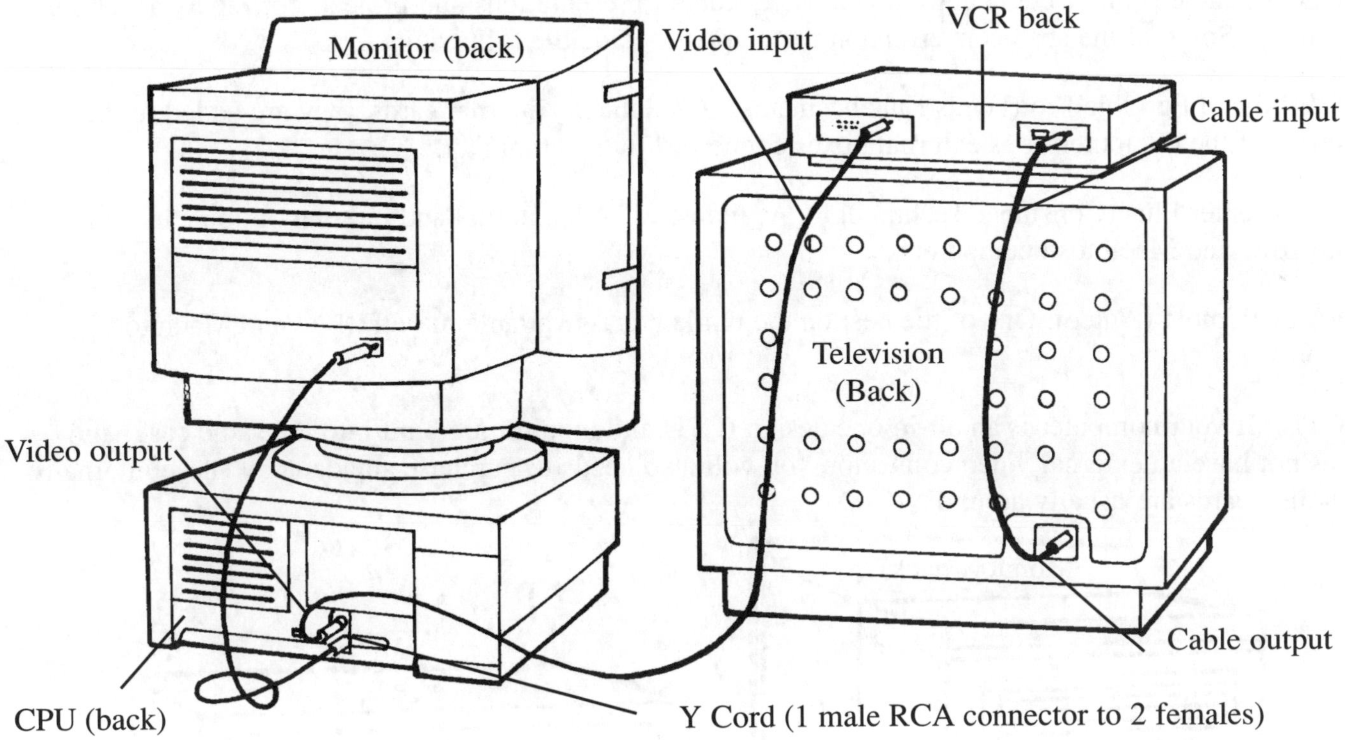

CONNECTING YOUR COMPUTER TO ANOTHER DISPLAY *(cont.)*

CONNECTING YOUR NEWER COMPUTER TO A TELEVISION

In order to accomplish the higher-resolution graphics common on today's computer, computer companies such as IBM and Apple had to move away from the line video used for television signals. Because of this, special hardware called a scan converter or print-to-video box is needed to convert these high-resolution video signals to those which can be handled by televisions. These boxes are fairly affordable, ranging in price from $150–$300. If televisions and VCRs are available, they give the user the added dimension of being able to videotape student presentations and projects for replay at school or home. Some of the scan convertors on the market include the following:

LTV Pro and Portable Pro (Focus Enhancements): Available as internal cards, they are added to the interior of the computer or as external boxes connected to the computer.

The Presenter Plus (Consumer Technology): Available in both external and internal options, it works on both IBM and Macintosh computers.

TVAtor Remote (Antec): One of the best on the market, it is available in both IBM and Macintosh formats.

NOTE: If your computer is an all-in-one design (CPU and monitor are built into the same case) and does not have an external video connector, you will also needs to purchase an adapter. These internally installed cards are usually around $75.00.

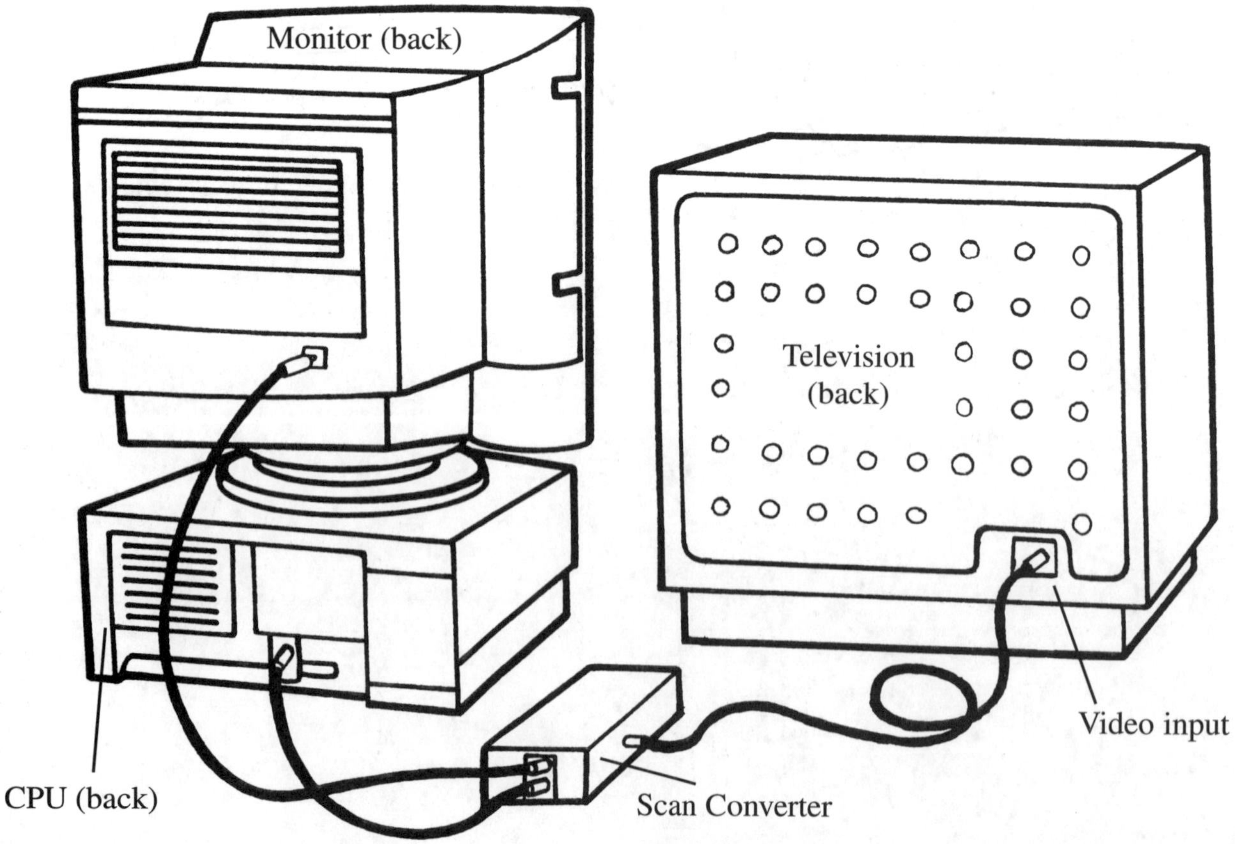

CONNECTING YOUR COMPUTER TO ANOTHER DISPLAY *(cont.)*

LCD PANEL

Liquid-crystal display panels, or LCD panels, work using the same technology as the digital watches many of us own. The difference is that the liquid crystals flow between two sheets of glass that are embedded with electrodes. This panel is then placed on an overhead projector connected to a computer and projected onto a large screen. These devices are still a little pricey for a single classroom and usually require a teacher to turn off the lights in the classroom, which all of us recognize is a no-no! In addition, most of these panels will require a special, extra-bright overhead projector, which is an additional cost. The most cost-effective use of an LCD panel is to share it among several teachers. Many suppliers will loan panels on a trial basis to schools that are interested in buying one.

CONNECTING YOUR COMPUTER TO ANOTHER DISPLAY *(cont.)*

LARGE-SCREEN PROJECTORS

The optimal but most expensive way to project a computer image is through a large-screen projection device. At one time, these machines were well over $10,000 but have steadily become smaller, brighter, and cheaper. Now you can buy a good quality large-screen projector which weighs less than ten pounds for under $4,000. Although that is still very expensive, many schools are trying to buy one or even two per building because of the fine quality of the images it projects.

These large-screen projectors can be used to project a computer image, a video, and a laserdisc onto a screen as small as a pulldown classroom screen and as large as a movie screen! A few people to hundreds of people can view the image of a computer screen when it is projected by a large-screen projector. Another advantage to this device is that the lights do not need to be completely dimmed, which is a huge bonus for classroom use.

Well-known brands of large-screen projectors include InFocus, Eiki, NEC, and Sony. Obviously, large-screen projectors are very costly; however, the hope is that it is only a matter of time before these devices become ubiquitous tools which empower the teacher in the classroom.

Slide Shows on the Computer—Paint Programs

Hopefully, you have figured out a good way to project your computer so a class of students can easily see it. It is unlikely that you will have a TV, LCD panel, or a large-screen projector permanently in your classroom; however, it is hopeful that you can borrow a projection device and use it in your classroom regularly. The next several pages will be devoted to teaching you how to make and present slide shows that are sure to motivate students, teachers, and parents. These slide shows could be used to launch a unit, show at Back-to-School Night, or highlight student work. In addition, ideas will be included for student-generated slide shows that can be used as visual aids for a culminating project.

Understanding the Different Presentation Software Available

Most presentation software available falls into two categories: paint programs and presentation programs. The division between these families is not always clear, though, as many paint programs have presentation capabilities and most presentation programs have paint programs built in. Paint programs such as *Kid Pix* are typically not as flexible when presenting information and, likewise, presentation programs such as *Power Point* are not as powerful in their art abilities. Nevertheless, both types of programs can be used to make first-class presentations for your classroom.

Paint Programs

A paint program, like crayons, watercolors, and pencils, is just another medium for teachers or students to express themselves through art. The difference is that this medium uses computer and monitor instead of paint and canvas. By manipulating different built-in tools, the teacher or student can "paint" pictures on a screen. These pictures can then be printed, electronically pasted into written projects, or used in presentations.

SLIDE SHOWS ON THE COMPUTER—PAINT PROGRAMS *(cont.)*

HOW DO YOU USE A PAINT PROGRAM?

Teachers:

Paint programs can be used for whole-class instruction of all curriculum areas by using a type of large-screen projection. The computer essentially becomes your chalkboard, allowing you to prepare drawings to display during class. Using the slide show option which is built into many paint programs, teachers can easily show progressions that are either difficult or impossible to show with a blackboard.

Students:

Students can use paint programs to draw illustrations for original stories or reports, make science observations, explore visual math and mapping skills, and hosts of other things. See the shapes slide show on the next few pages done by a primary student using *Kid Pix Studio*. This would be an excellent learning center project and one to highlight at Back-to-School Night. Step-by-step directions for this shape slide show can be found on pages 48–49.

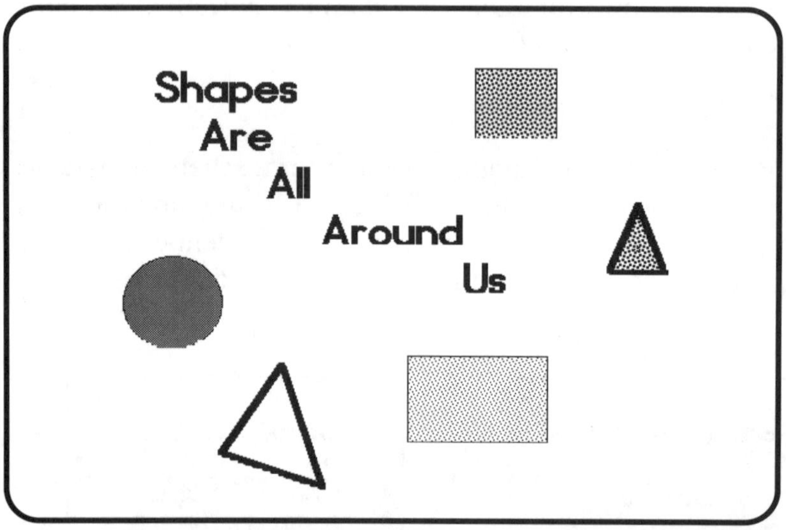

SLIDE SHOWS ON THE COMPUTER—PAINT PROGRAMS *(cont.)*

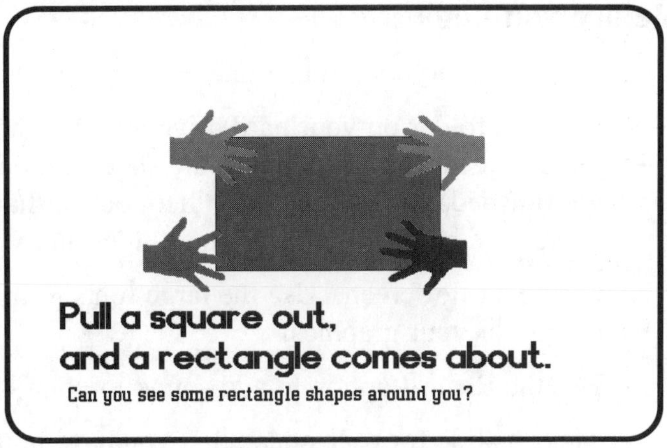

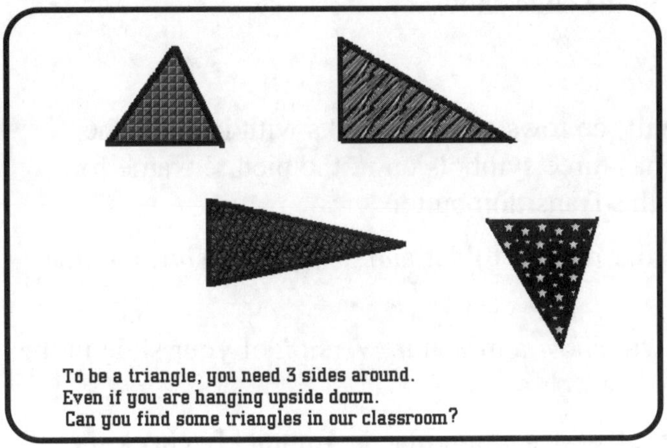

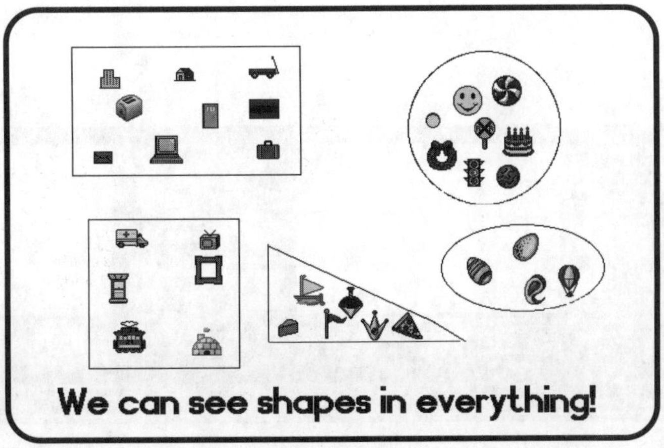

Slide Shows on the Computer—Paint Programs *(cont.)*

Shapes Are All Around Us—Kid Pix Slide Show Directions

Before you begin:

Use one of the storyboard blackline masters found on pages 50–51 to plan your slide show.

- Create a folder on your hard drive into which you will place all the slides for your slide show. If you are using *Kid Pix Studio,* the slides are automatically saved into the KPS folder. When you are finished, you need to drag them out of that folder and put them in your own folder. It just makes life easier to work from a folder that you have labeled Slide Show Shapes.
- Create a title screen. Use the large fonts to make it clearer on the screen. Use lots of contrasting colors for your graphics.
- Use the Record option to add sound to your slides.
- Make a slide for each shape that you have taught. Add a sound.
- After you have created each slide, save it on the hard drive. Be sure to name it so that you know what is on that slide when you are ready to put it in the slide show.

Making Slides:

If you are using *Kid Pix* to make this slide show, you will see rows of three trucks with icons at the bottom when using the slide show feature. Each truck has three symbols on it: the picture frame for "Pick a Slide"; the music note for "Pick a Sound"; and the Transition button.

- Click on the Pick a Slide button. It should open your disk or folder and display the slides in that folder.
- Click on the slide you want and then select it. It will show a miniature version of your slide in the truck.
- Select the slides for each consecutive "truck" until all slides are in place. To quickly check the order of the slides, press the Play button at the bottom of the screen.

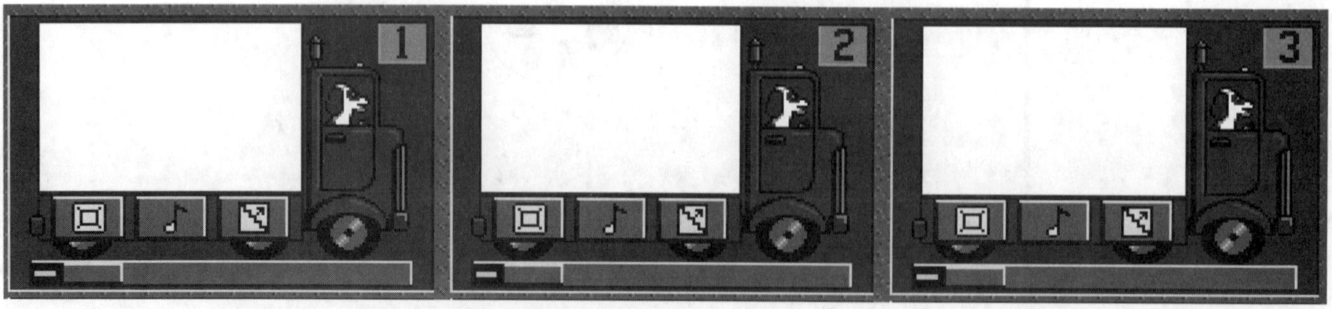

SLIDE SHOWS ON THE COMPUTER—PAINT PROGRAMS *(cont.)*

SHAPES ARE ALL AROUND US—KID PIX SLIDE SHOW DIRECTIONS *(cont.)*

- Next click on the Pick a Sound button. Choose the sound you want and click Select. If you recorded in *Kid Pix,* that recording will automatically be chosen unless you tell it otherwise. If you want to record in slide show, click on the music note and click on the microphone. Record as you would in Kid Pix. Click on Save and then Select. You cannot have more than one sound on a slide unless you put the slide in more than one truck.
- Now choose your transition. Click on the transition button. Choose the one you want and then click Select. (The dissolve and the cut transitions are best when creating animation).
- When you finish, go to the File menu and select Save As. Name your slide show and click Save.
- You can choose a background color for your slide show by going into the Goodies menu and selecting Background Color.
- To play your slide show, go to the Goodies menu and select Play Once or click the play button at the bottom of the screen. To play the slide show over and over, go to the Goodies menu and select Play Looped. This will play your slide show until the mouse is double-clicked.

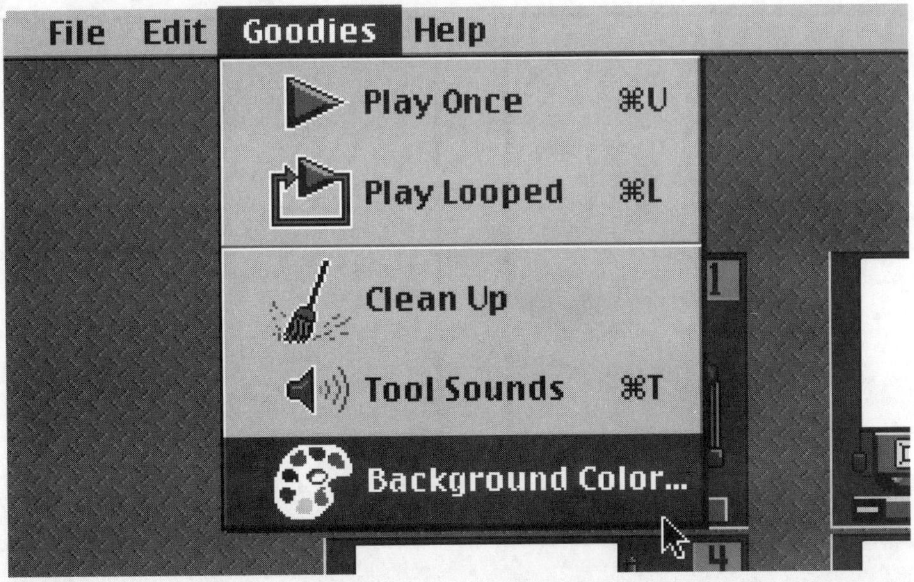

SLIDE SHOWS ON THE COMPUTER—PAINT PROGRAMS *(cont.)*

SLIDE SHOW STORYBOARD 1

Slide # ____________

Words/Narration ______________________________

____

____

____

____

____

Slide # ____________

Words/Narration ______________________________

____

____

____

____

____

Slide # ____________

Words/Narration ______________________________

____

____

____

____

____

Slide # ____________

Words/Narration ______________________________

____

____

____

____

____

Slide Shows on the Computer—Paint Programs *(cont.)*

Slide Show Storyboard 2

Slide # __________

Slide # __________

Slide # __________

Slide # __________

SLIDE SHOWS ON THE COMPUTER—PRESENTATION PROGRAMS

HOW DO YOU USE A PRESENTATION PROGRAM?

Everyone learns differently whether by the audible, visual, or written word. Presentation programs empower the teacher to reach a variety of learning styles by allowing the teachers and students to use multimedia (text, art, sounds, graphics, animation, and video) to demonstrate their knowledge of a subject. Instead of pages in a written report, the user creates slides that are linked to one another. The user places different types of media on these slides to communicate particular ideas. The output can be printed; however, usually these presentations are designed to be viewed with an interacting audience using the computer. *HyperStudio* and *PowerPoint* are two of the most popular presentation programs.

Teachers:

The chalkboard is an invaluable tool for teachers. Its drawback is that it is limited to static, two-dimensional drawings and text. Presentation programs allow the teacher to go beyond the chalkboard to present lessons that come alive with pictures, drawings, animation, movies, sounds, and text. The computer becomes an electronic chalkboard full of color, motion, and sound.

Beginner Project:

Do you ever stand in front of a group of parents at Back-to-School Night who look rather bored and simply attend because of pressure from their kids? Using a presentation program like *HyperStudio* or *PowerPoint* is an excellent way to make your presentation come alive. All of us are trying to communicate certain themes, values, and strategies at Back-to-School Night. Below you will find an example of a Back-to-School Night presentation done in *PowerPoint*. This same project is found on the CD-ROM in template form.

SLIDE SHOWS ON THE COMPUTER—PRESENTATION PROGRAMS *(cont.)*

BACK-TO-SCHOOL NIGHT

***PowerPoint* Presentation** *(cont.)*

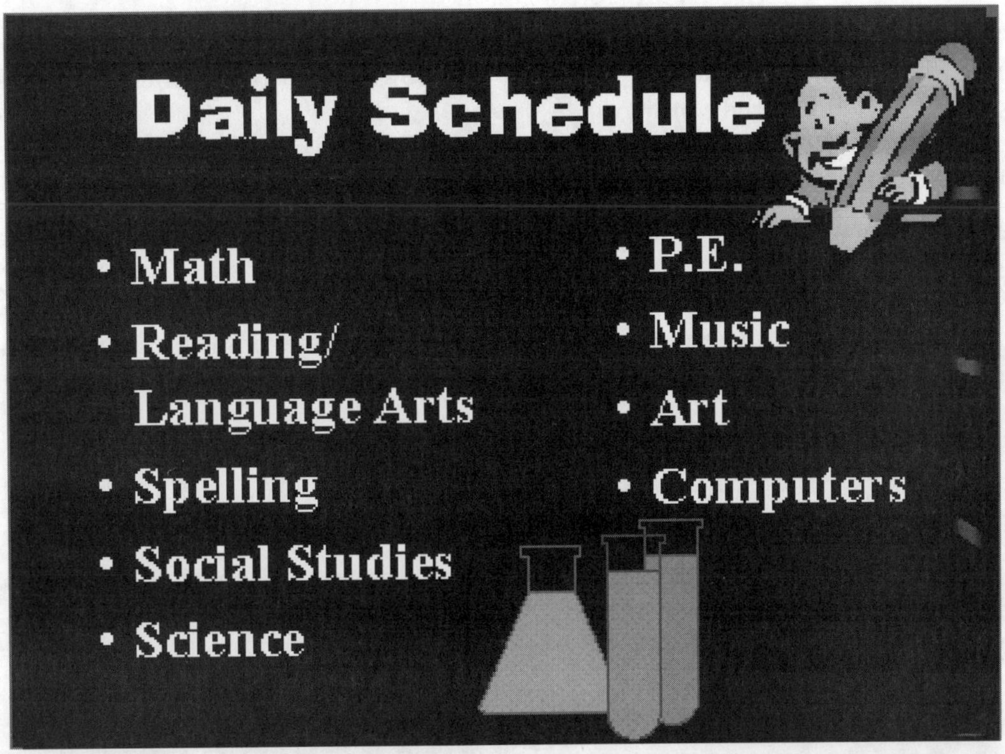

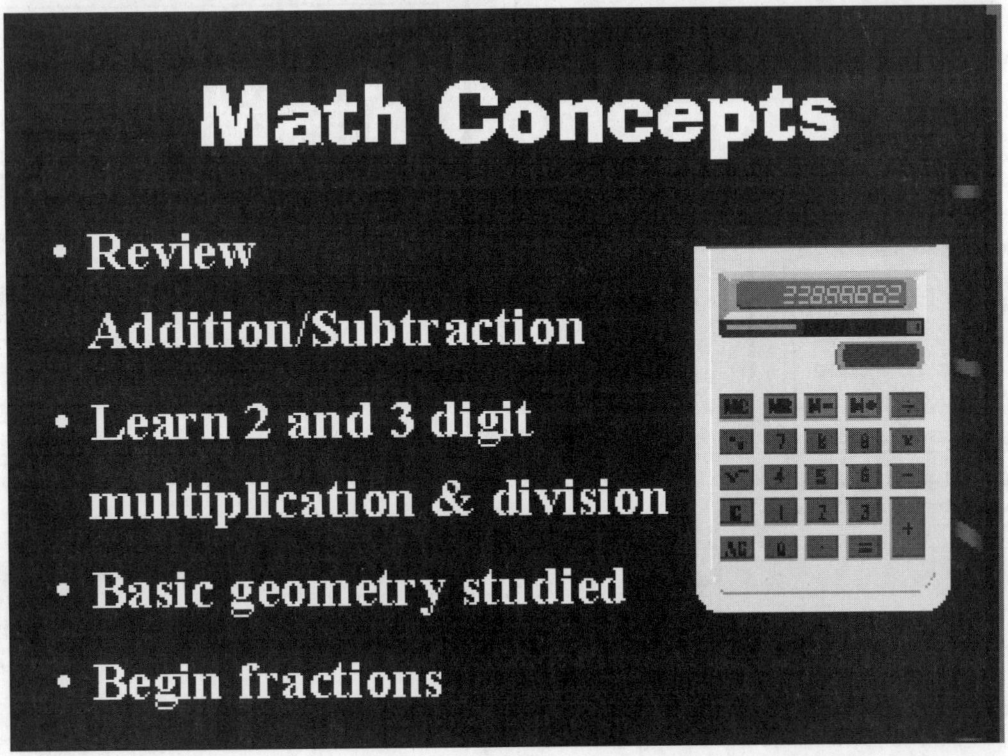

SLIDE SHOWS ON THE COMPUTER—PRESENTATION PROGRAMS (cont.)

BACK-TO-SCHOOL NIGHT

PowerPoint Presentation Directions

If you are a beginning user of *PowerPoint,* you may want to begin by using the template on the CD-ROM. However, the following directions will show you how to start from scratch in *PowerPoint* to complete this Back-to-School Night project.

How to Create Your *PowerPoint* Presentation:

- Use one of the storyboard blackline masters found on pages 50–51 to plan your slide show.
- Open *PowerPoint* and choose a template (slide background). Decide which layout you want.
- Type your information in the boxes. When you are typing your points beside the bullets, it is very important to NOT press Enter or Return at the end of the line unless you want a new bullet.
- Add clip art by clicking on Insert, Picture, and then Clip Art.
- Continue adding new slides by clicking on Insert, New Slide. You may choose a different layout; however, your template (slide background) should stay the same for all of the slides.
- To change the font style, color, or size, first highlight the text. Then use the toolbars at the top and bottom to change the font.
- Spell check your presentation.

Slide Shows on the Computer—Presentation Programs *(cont.)*

Back-to-School Night

PowerPoint Presentation Directions *(cont.)*

Displaying Your *PowerPoint* Presentation:

- Once you have finished creating your *PowerPoint* presentation, you will want to view it on a full screen. To do this, click on View and then Slide Show.
- To make transitions between slides, click on View and then Slide Sorter. On the toolbar, you will see "No Transition." Click on the pulldown menu and choose a transition. Test it by clicking on View and then Slide Show.
- To make the written items on each slide appear one at a time, click on View, Slide Sorter. On the toolbar, you will see "No Effect." Choose an effect for the way you want the written items to appear. Test it by clicking on View and then Slide Show.
- Once you are pleased with your entire slide show, save it. Attach your computer to a TV or another type of projection device and get ready to dazzle your parents at Back-to-School Night!

Other *PowerPoint* Ideas:

PowerPoint is a wonderful program because once you become proficient at using the program, it is a quick and easy way to make professional presentations. Students can also create simple *PowerPoint* slide shows as a culminating project. A teacher may want to put students in teams and have them do a slide show together. *PowerPoint* is also ideal for making certificates, handouts, and book covers, as shown below and on the next page.

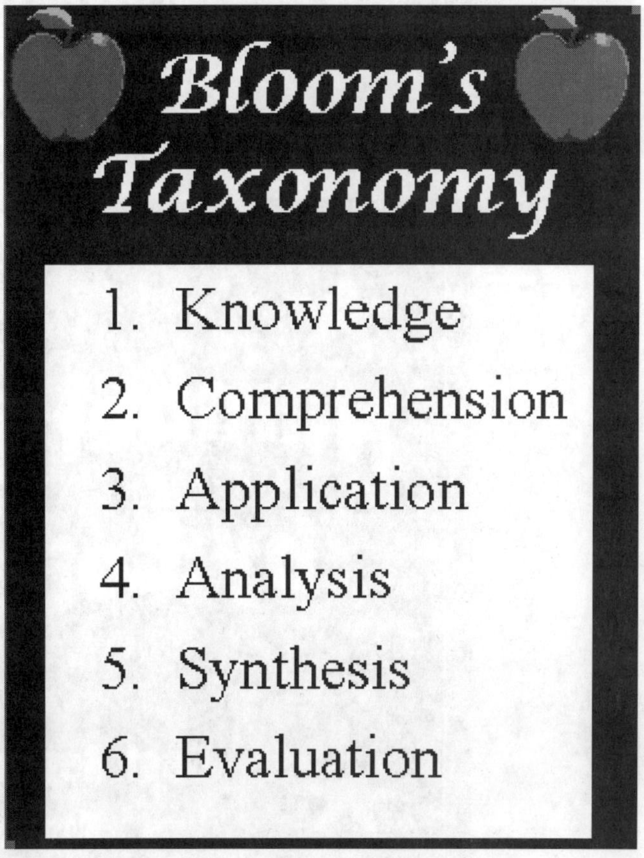

SLIDE SHOWS ON THE COMPUTER—PRESENTATION PROGRAMS *(cont.)*

Other *PowerPoint* Ideas *(cont.)*

Certificate Example

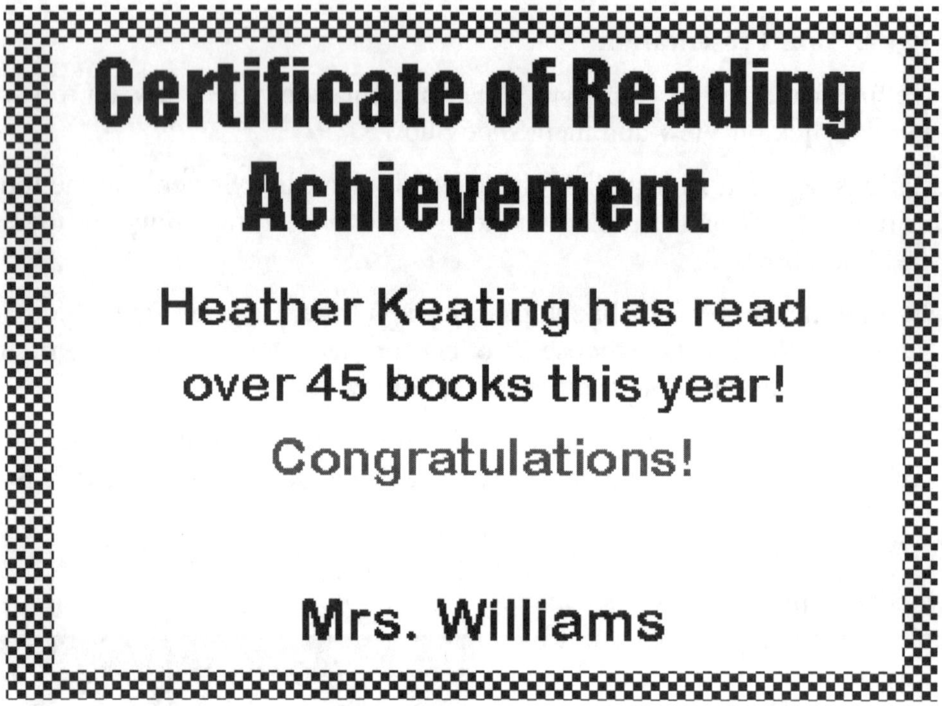

Book Cover Example

SLIDE SHOWS ON THE COMPUTER—MULTIMEDIA PROGRAMS

USING HYPERSTUDIO

HyperStudio is a dynamic and exciting multimedia software programs that is finding a place in school across the continent. Outstanding presentations can be made by teachers and students using *HyperStudio*. Becoming familiar with this program will take some time, but the rewards are many. There is no way that in a few pages one can learn *HyperStudio;* however, there are many books available that will walk you step-by-step through the program if you are unfamiliar with *HyperStudio.* Suggested books include *HyperStudio for Terrified Teachers* or *HyperStudio: Simple Projects,* both published by Teacher Created Materials.

The main idea of *HyperStudio* is to create cards (or slides) which are connected by buttons. A person who is creating a *HyperStudio* stack should design the cards on paper first, which is called storyboarding. You will find storyboard cards on pages 50–51. Storyboards enable a teacher to manage student projects easily because the complete design process is done on paper, not at the computer. The cards that you or your students create should contain one or more of the following:

- text
- clip art
- photos (digital camera, Internet, or scanned)
- video
- sound
- animation

The tools in *HyperStudio* can be manipulated to perform a number of artistic tasks. Below is an example of a typical toolbox used in *HyperStudio*.

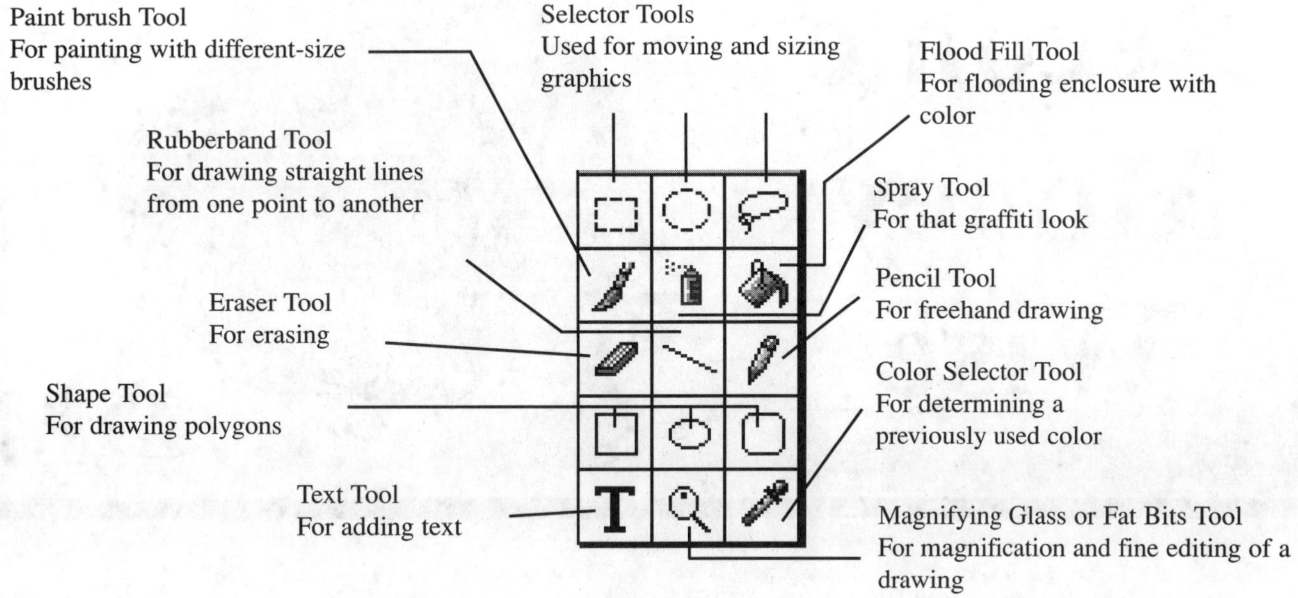

SLIDE SHOWS ON THE COMPUTER—MULTIMEDIA PROGRAMS *(cont.)*

EXAMPLES OF HYPERSTUDIO TEACHER PROJECTS

Because of their interactivity, presentation programs can be used for customized, individual instruction. Small groups or individuals can view or interact with teacher-developed lessons at a computer station. If the teacher uses a presentation to teach the class certain skills, he or she can then use the presentation at a computer station for independent, individualized instruction of students who were absent during a lesson or of those needing extra reinforcement. This allows all the students to be served more efficiently as the teacher is able to continue with the next lesson while the computer offers the remediation. In addition, the teacher can easily save and archive the computer lesson for future years.

Below is an example of a *HyperStudio* stack created by a teacher to reinforce money-counting skills with her students. The teacher created this stack to be used at a learning center. Students would rotate to the computer, and the goal would be to get every student on the computer within one week.

SLIDE SHOWS ON THE COMPUTER—MULTIMEDIA PROGRAMS *(cont.)*

EXAMPLES OF HYPERSTUDIO TEACHER PROJECTS *(cont.)*

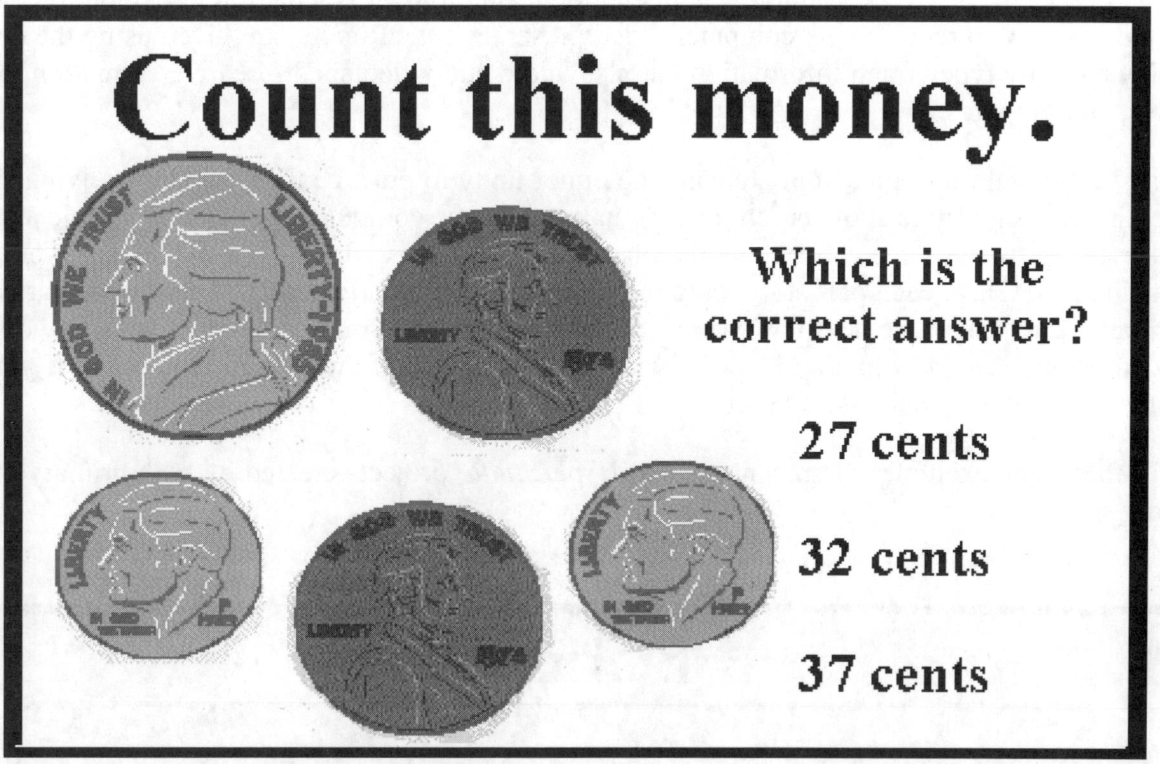

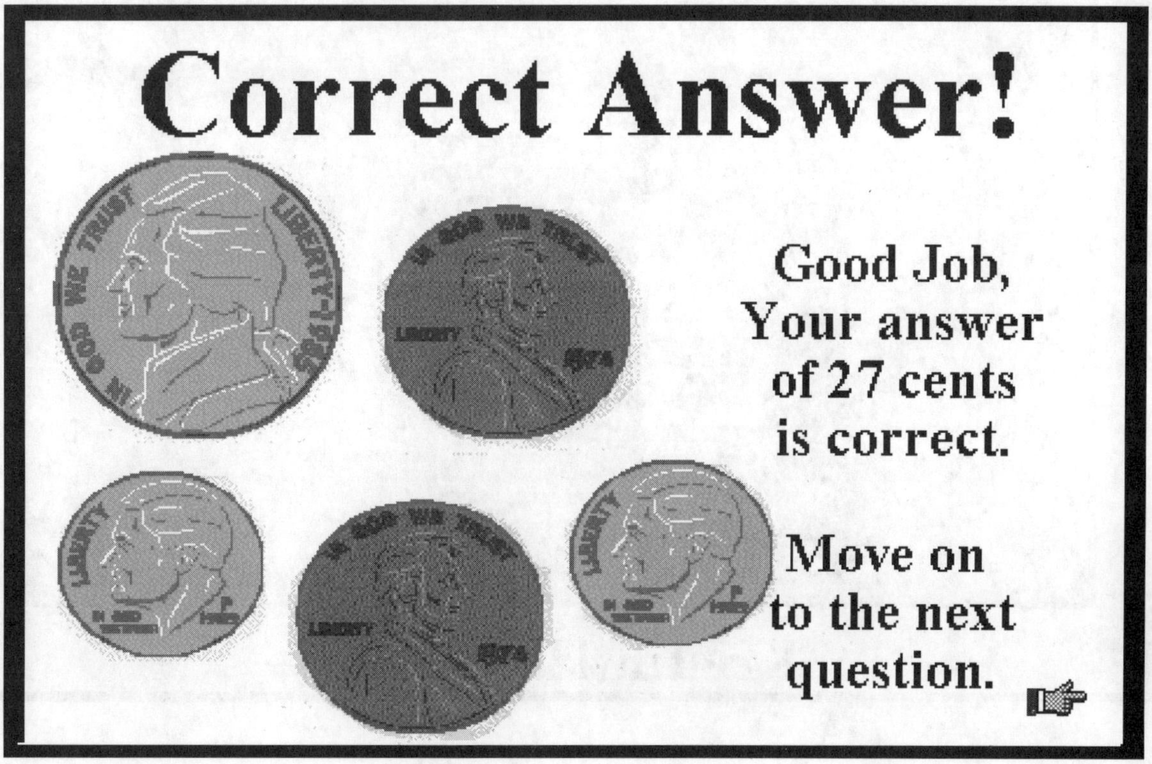

SLIDE SHOWS ON THE COMPUTER—MULTIMEDIA PROGRAMS *(cont.)*

EXAMPLES OF HYPERSTUDIO STUDENT PROJECTS

After the teacher becomes comfortable with using the technology, it is a natural transition to begin to teach students how to report using computer-aided presentations. Reports are given using the computer to display not only typewritten information but also audio and videotaped research, animation, photos, drawings, and graphics.

You may find it helpful to give your students the opportunity to practice their problem-solving skills involved in creating a slide show before they actually go to the computer. Give them a topic and have them storyboard two or three cards using the blank cards on pages 50–51. You may want to put students in pairs. Have each pair storyboard their presentations (start small!). Then rotate partners to the computer throughout the next few weeks, giving each pair a 30-minute block of time to work. Many computers have built-in alarm clocks that can be set to go off after an allotted time. If your computer does not have one, use a timer.

You will find some examples of student-created *HyperStudio* projects created by both primary children and older students.

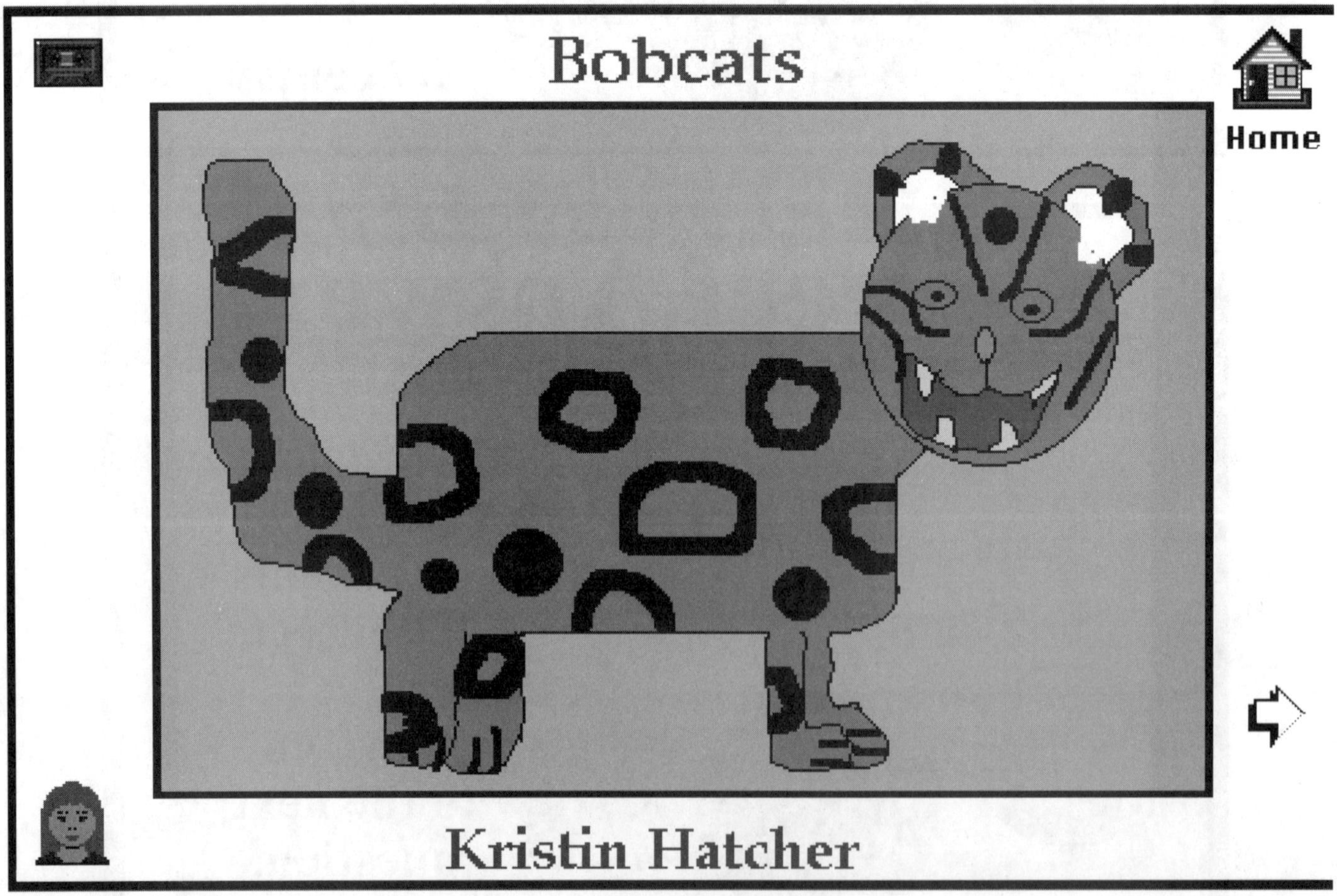

SLIDE SHOWS ON THE COMPUTER—MULTIMEDIA PROGRAMS *(cont.)*

EXAMPLES OF HYPERSTUDIO STUDENT PROJECTS *(cont.)*

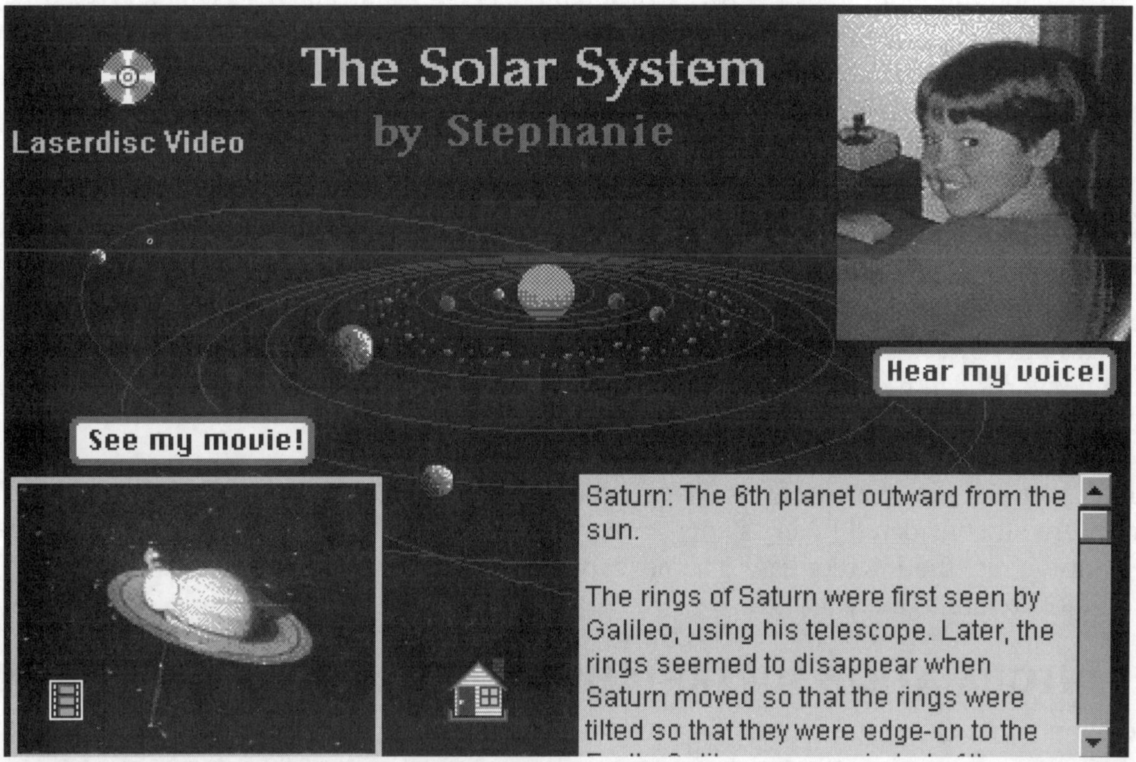

THE INTERNET—WHAT, HOW AND WHY?

WHAT IS THE INTERNET?

The Internet is nothing more than a network of interconnected electronic data which crisscrosses and zigzags over miles and miles of phone line, creating a "web." These computers communicate through satellite, buried fiber optic cable, telephone lines, and other data links. All computers can connect regardless of their hardware brand. Your Macintosh can communicate with a Windows machine anywhere in the world without a problem.

HISTORY OF THE INTERNET

The Internet was created in 1983 with 100 networks and has grown by leaps and bounds. By 1993, there were approximately 10,000 networks attached to the Internet. Most experts believe the number of networks currently attached to the Internet is well into the hundreds of thousands. Since each of the connected networks can be as many as tens of thousand of computers, the total number of individual users of the Internet is easily over 35 million.

If you think you will not be part of this change, look at history. The telegraph, telephone, and television were all considered luxury items at one time, and not one of these inventions has grown in popularity at the rate the Internet has. The next five years will create a paradigm shift in the way we and our schools relate to the world.

IS THE INFORMATION SUPERHIGHWAY THE SAME AS THE INTERNET?

The Internet is often called the information superhighway. Just as a highway has several lanes to travel, as well as many options along the way, on-ramps, off-ramps, loops, and other connecting highways, the information superhighway offers the same kind of situation to computer users. As our society and school systems shift from the industrial age to the information age, the information superhighway is a powerful, necessary tool.

Drivers on the superhighway have access to virtually unlimited information. Online libraries, museums, e-mail, newspapers, magazines, and professional forums are available to any user. Today's information superhighway is alive with graphics, sound, video, and animation.

THE WORLD WIDE WEB

The World Wide Web (WWW) is the fastest growing segment of the Internet. Simply put, the Web is a series of interconnected documents and pages. Using the World Wide Web is like using a superlibrary, if you will. You can move from site to site, from document to document, from page to film clip, from sound clip to document with simply the click on the mouse—thus, a World Wide Web of connection. The reason for the Web's overwhelming success is its ease of navigation and its media-rich environment. Early Internet users had to input long strings of text that would direct them to their destination compared to the simple point-and-click feature of today's modern browsers.

THE INTERNET—WHAT, HOW AND WHY? *(cont.)*

WHAT DO I NEED TO GET ON THE INTERNET?

In most cases, for you and your students to get online, you will need four pieces of equipment:

Computer

Almost any current PC or Macintosh will allow you to get online.

Modem

Your modem is the peripheral device that allows your computer to communicate with other computers via a telephone line. If your computer is only a year or two old, chances are it came with a built-in modem. If not, you can buy an external modem that attaches to your computer. Your modem speed must be 14.4 bps or better to successfully access the Internet. Modem speeds continue to improve, and new computers should have a modem speed of 33.6 bps or better. The faster the modem speed, the faster the information from the Internet will appear on your monitor as you are downloading it.

Phone Line

A basic phone line dedicated to one computer is preferable. The line should have touch-tone dialing rather than rotary and should not have a call-waiting feature added. If your school has a direct connection to the Internet, you will not need a modem or a phone line.

Telecommunication Software

You will need a software package not only to connect you to the Internet but also to be able to view and navigate through the Internet. Today nearly all of the software you need is provided in one software package. Browser software like *Netscape Navigator* or *Internet Explorer* both have all of the software you need to use the Internet. Commercial online services like America Online or Prodigy offer a network and Web browser all in one. Thus, you would not need any extra software with a commercial online service.

THE INTERNET—WHAT, HOW AND WHY? (cont.)

WHY SHOULD I USE THE INTERNET IN MY CLASSROOM?

The Internet gives teachers and students access to information of a quality and quantity never seen before in education. Using the Internet allows the user to retrieve information, media, and even software from all over the world almost instantaneously.

But gathering information is merely one aspect of the power of the Internet—communication is the other. Once you have access to the Internet, you have access to all the users of the Internet—teachers sharing and collaborating with other teachers, students with other students, students with scientists, and the list goes on. Distances, classes, races, and cultures are no longer barriers to the sharing of ideas.

Some of the most popular uses of the Internet by teachers and students include the following:

- Gathering information on almost any subject
- Communicating with others via e-mail
- Joining discussion groups on a specific topic
- Finding valuable lesson plans and activities
- Publishing students' work online
- Utilizing government information which is not easily accessible by the general public
- Communicating with experts in any field
- Taking part in electronic expeditions

THE INTERNET—RULES AND REGULATIONS

THE RULES OF THE INFORMATION SUPERHIGHWAY

Just as there are behaviors that are acceptable at school, students need to learn the correct procedure and rules for using the Internet. This powerful educational tool is a privilege. It can provide countless hours of exploration and use, but like a driver's license, it is a privilege that can be taken away for breaking the rules. Below is a list of basic Internet rules. It would be a good idea to discuss these rules with your students and to post them near the classroom computer.

1. I WILL NOT GIVE OUT PERSONAL INFORMATION SUCH AS MY ADDRESS, TELEPHONE NUMBER, OR NAME AND LOCATION OF MY SCHOOL WITHOUT CHECKING WITH MY TEACHER FIRST.

2. I WILL TELL MY TEACHER IMMEDIATELY IF I COME ACROSS ANY INFORMATION THAT MAKES ME FEEL UNCOMFORTABLE.

3. I WILL NEVER SEND A PERSON MY PICTURE OR ANY OTHER PICTURE WITHOUT FIRST CHECKING WITH MY PARENTS.

4. IF I AM USING INFORMATION FROM THE INTERNET FOR A REPORT, I WILL PUT THE INFORMATION IN MY OWN WORDS. I WILL NOT PLAGIARIZE INFORMATION FROM THE INTERNET.

5. I WILL BE CAREFUL ABOUT COPYRIGHTS AND ALWAYS CITE MY SOURCES IN THE BIBLIOGRAPHY.

6. I WILL NEVER AGREE TO "MEET" SOMEONE ONLINE WITHOUT FIRST CHECKING WITH MY TEACHER.

THE INTERNET—RULES AND REGULATIONS *(cont.)*

GAINING PARENT SUPPORT AND PERMISSION

Since many of the activities available on the Internet can be done outside of school hours, parents will need to assume supervision of their child's use of the Internet, too. Many districts have an Acceptable Use Policy that parents are required to sign indicating that they know the school's policy on general computer usage and specific Internet use. A presentation at a teacher-parent meeting might be a good time for you to communicate to parents the value of having the Internet as a resource in today's world of education. General parental cooperation is an important component for any successful Internet experience. Below you will find Web site addresses which you will find helpful if you want to construct an AUP.

Sample Acceptable Use Policies
http://www.usoe.k12.ut.us/curr/Internet/aup/aupdir.html

K-12 Acceptable Use Policies
http://www.erehwon.com/k12aup/

Dear Parents,

We are fortunate to provide the most current electronic resources for our students. With your permission, our class will be exploring the Internet to gather valuable information related to various topics throughout the year. Please note that we will not be visiting "chat" rooms. All of the Internet sites have been previewed and deemed suitable for young learners. Each Internet activity will be supervised by an adult. At no time will the students be allowed to have free access to the Internet.

Please sign this form to grant permission for your child to use Internet resources and return it to school. We welcome you to join us one day to experience this extraordinary opportunity (days and times to be determined). Thank you for supporting our efforts to provide the most exciting educational opportunity for our students!

Sincerely,

______ I give my child ____________________________ permission to work on the Internet.

______ I **DO NOT** wish my child to work on the Internet.

Signed: ____

THE INTERNET—RULES AND REGULATIONS *(cont.)*

SAFE SURFING

Because the Internet is a public forum, free speech is more than a right—it is the rule. Nearly anyone can publish almost anything on it. We must acknowledge the fact that there is inappropriate material on the Internet and then do everything we can to actively avoid this material. Students should know that accessing any such material in any form is strictly prohibited.

As mentioned on the previous page, constructing an Acceptable Use Policy is a good place to start in order to encourage safe Internet surfing in your classroom. These AUPs should clearly define the rules and responsibilities of using the Internet and should be distributed to all students.

In addition to having an AUP in place, here are a few general rules to encourage safe Internet surfing in your classroom.

- Supervision, supervision, supervision. Keep an eye on students while they are using the Internet.
- Take time to teach students to be responsible when on the Internet and show them appropriate sites to visit.
- Create a list of appropriate educational sites and bookmark these on your computer.

THE INTERNET—RULES AND REGULATIONS *(cont.)*

SAFE SURFING *(cont.)*

Net Monitoring Software

There are several products on the market that help you block inappropriate information from appearing on your computer. A few of the more popular products are listed below. All of these can be downloaded in demo form for no charge from the Internet. Many demos will work for a month and then disable themselves.

Name: *Cyber Patrol*

Product Description: *Cyber Patrol* is used to manage Internet access, limit the total time spent online, and block access to sites deemed as inappropriate.

Download Demo Copy at: http://www.microsys.com/cyber

Name: *Net Nanny*

Product Description: *Net Nanny* allows YOU to monitor, screen, and block access to anything residing on, running in, out, or through your computer, online or offline. It's two-way screening in real-time, and only you determine what is screened with the help of the site list.

Download Demo Copy at: http://www.netnanny.com/

Name: *SurfWatch*

Product Description: *SurfWatch* blocks tens of thousands of inappropriate sites locally at the user's machine without restricting the access rights of other Internet users. Monthly updates are provided to *SurfWatch* users, containing the most recent list of blocked sites.

Download Demo Copy at: http://www.surfwatch.com

PUBLISHING STUDENT WORK ON THE INTERNET

COPYRIGHT CONCERNS

Because the Internet is still a somewhat new medium in the public's hands, there are several gray areas surrounding copyrights. Almost everything is copyrighted the minute it is written. No copyright notice is required. As much as possible, your students should paraphrase and give attribution, which is a good writing practice anyway. As long as you are using an article for educational purposes and not selling it, you may use the information. However, it is important to cite all Internet references at all times. To be safe, ask permission from the Web sites from which you are using information. It is usually just a matter of sending a quick e-mail message and waiting for a response. See page 175 for how to cite Internet sources.

GUIDELINES FOR PUBLISHING WORK ON THE INTERNET

The remarkable thing about the Internet is that it can provide a global audience for student work. There are several Internet sites listed below that allow students to post projects. These sites sometimes allow students to post photos of themselves with their work. Before you attempt this, you should have a signed release from parents. A sample release form is provided for you on the next page. You will also want to check with your school to see if a procedure is in place for this type of thing. If there is no standard release form at your school, have the administration check the release form you are considering before you use it.

Name: *Kid Pub*

Description: *Kid Pub* is a wonderful place to publish student stories or poems on the Internet. Both younger and older students can publish their work, and all submitted stories are published. The Web master chooses his favorites and puts them in a special section.

Address: http://www.kidpub.org/kidpub

Name: *CyberKids* and *CyberTeens*

Description: Young people all over the world make *CyberKids* and *CyberTeens* a sharing, caring place for kids. Students' creativity can flourish while they get feedback from others, read stories, post stories, listen to kids' musical compositions, view artwork, and much more.

Address: http://www.cyberkids.com

Name: *Young Writers*

Description: The Young Writer's Resource Page is full of annotated links including writers' guidelines, writing contests, and online writing.

Address: http://www.inkspot.com/young

PUBLISHING STUDENT WORK ON THE INTERNET *(cont.)*

Example of a Release Form

Dear Parents/Guardians,

We are excited to let you know that our class will be publishing our work on the Internet. This means that anyone in the world who has access to the Internet will be able to view your child's work. The potential audience is in the millions, and we hope this includes your family and friends.

Your signature below grants permission for your child's work to be published on the Internet.

Sincerely,

Classroom Teacher

☐ My child's work, which may be accompanied by his/her first name, may be electronically displayed and produced.

☐ My child's work, which may not be accompanied by his/her first name, may be electronically displayed and produced.

☐ Photographs of my child, which may be accompanied by his/her first name, may be electronically displayed and produced.

☐ Photographs of my child, which may not be accompanied by his/her first name, may be electronically displayed and produced.

I hereby give the above permission and release ______________________________ from any liability resulting from or connected with the publication of my child's work.

______________________________	______________________________
Child's Name	Teacher
______________________________	______________________________
Parent/Guardian Signature	Date

INTERNET VOCABULARY

Before using the Internet in your classroom, a basic understanding of Internet vocabulary is crucial for success. Many of these terms will be used throughout the next several pages. You will want to copy, laminate, and post this page near the computer.

Browser	Software which allows you to access and browse the World Wide Web. (Popular browser software includes *Netscape Navigator* and *Microsoft Internet Explorer*)
Bookmark	Marking a page so in the future you can go directly to this marked Web page without typing the Web address every time
Domain	The Internet name for a particular computer network or system, these are indicated in an Internet address by the designations .edu, .org, .gov, .com, etc. If the Internet address has a domain of .gov, then it would be a government site such as http://www.whitehouse.gov.
Download	To transfer data (usually text, software, or graphics) from another computer
E-mail	Short for electronic mail
Hits	Common term for the number of matches found when doing an Internet search
Home Page	First screen viewed when visiting a Web site
HTML	Programming language of the World Wide Web
HTTP	HTTP stands for hypertext transfer protocol; it is the method by which a Web page is accessed through the Internet.
Hyperlink	A link from one document to another, these links are usually represented by highlighted and/or underlined words or images that can be clicked. When using an Internet browser, usually the user can know if something is a hyperlink because the pointer will turn to a hand

INTERNET VOCABULARY *(cont.)*

Hypertext	A document format that feature links to other documents in the form of graphics, text, sound, and movies
Log Off	To disconnect your computer from communicating with another computer
Log On	To connect your computer to another computer, usually requires a password for identification
Modem	Device that uses communication lines to connect one computer to distant computers
Quicktime	Method of storing movies and audio files in a digital format developed by Apple Computer.
Search Engine	A way to search on the Internet similar to a card catalog (Some popular search engines include Alta Vista, Excite, Infoseek, and Yahoo!)
Shareware	Software that can be used on a trial basis before paying for it (Shareware can be found on the Internet at http://www.shareware.com.)
URL	URL stands for Uniform Resource Locator. A URL is another name for a Web site address, such as http://www.redcross.org.
Web page	A page on the World Wide Web may contain text, graphics, still and moving images, and sounds linked to other Web pages by hyperlinks.
WWW	WWW stands for the World Wide Web, also known as the Web. The WWW is the part of the Internet populated by millions of hypertext documents that are accessible by using an Internet browser.

INTERNET TIPS

HOW TO LAUNCH A WEB SITE ADDRESS

You've seen advertisements for a company's Web site on the television or in a magazine, such as for *USA Today* at http://www.usatoday.com. If you know the URL, or Web site address, then type the address at the top of the task bar and press the return key as shown in the example below. This will launch this particular Web site. You must type the exact Web site address, including all letters, numbers, punctuation, and symbols. If you do not type it correctly, it will not launch the Web site and you will get an error message.

USING A SEARCH ENGINE

Often you want to research a topic and do not know a particular Web site address. When this is the case, then you should use a search engine. A search engine is similar to a card catalog in the library. If you wanted to find a book in the library about lung cancer, you would not walk up and down the aisles in the library. You would first consult the card catalog which would direct you to the most appropriate place to find the book. A search engine is similar in that it assists you in finding information about a particular subject among the millions of pages on the Internet.

There are several popular search engines on the Internet. Some of the best search engines include the following:

Alta Vista	http://www.altavista.com
Excite	http://www.excite.com
Infoseek	http://infoseek.go.com/
Yahoo!	http://www.yahoo.com

INTERNET TIPS *(cont.)*

SEARCH ENGINES FOR KIDS

A popular kid's search engine that is simpler to use and has an excellent help section is called Yahooligans!

Yahooligans! http://www.yahooligans.com

HOW TO FIND A PARTICULAR TOPIC WHEN USING A SEARCH ENGINE

Once you have launched a search engine, it is rather easy to find information on your topic. Simply type your subject matter in the box provided on the home page of any search engine. If you want to find information about lung cancer, then you would type those words in the box provided. The engine would then search for any article containing the word "lung" or "cancer" in an article. The problem with this type of search is that you will get hundreds of articles dealing with lung and hundreds of articles dealing with cancer, but only some will actually be about "lung cancer." To narrow the search, put quotation marks around the words that act as one topic as shown below. Now the engine will only find articles with the phrase "lung cancer."

INTERNET TIPS *(cont.)*

BOOKMARKING YOUR FAVORITE WEB SITES

Bookmarking, simply stated, is a creating a link to a Web pages so one does not need to type the address when wanting to visit this same Web site in the future. When you are trying to type Web site addresses, all you need to do is make one small mistake for the address not to work. Bookmarking is a good technique to use with students, especially younger ones, because it is basically error free. Follow these steps below to make bookmarks of your own on the Internet.

- First, launch the site you want—see page 73 for more information on this.
- Once you are viewing the site you want, click on **Bookmark** from the tool bar and drag down to **Add a Bookmark.**

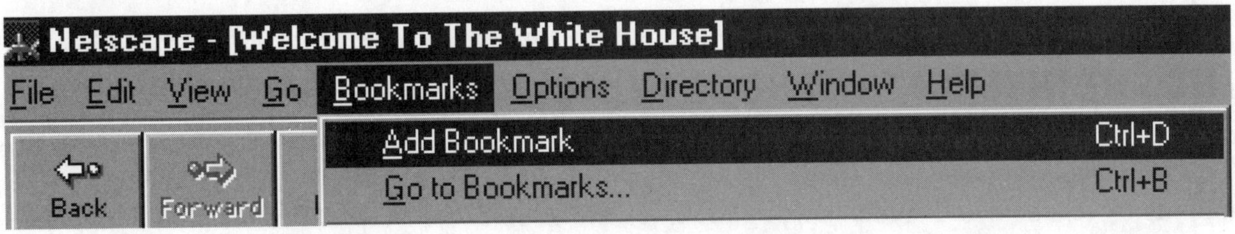

- Your bookmark will now appear in a list under the word **Bookmark** on the tool bar.
- To go to a site that you have bookmarked, click on **Bookmark** and drag down to the name of the site. If the site name is not on this list, try these steps again.

BE PATIENT

Downloading a page with numerous graphics takes up a lot of bandwidth. Large graphics may take some time to fully load, depending on the speed of the modem, the amount of the traffic on the server, and other factors outside of your control.

Try visiting the site prior to engaging the class. Connect to all of the links you intend to visit. When you return to the same site within a reasonable amount of time, the computer will cache, or store, some or all of the graphics onto your hard drive. This will accelerate downloading time.

Text portions of Web pages usually arrive much quicker than the accompanying graphics. Arrow down the page and read the text while the graphics are downloading. Then arrow back up the page and view the graphics.

INTERNET TIPS *(cont.)*

MAKE SURE THE INFORMATION IS ACCURATE

Encourage your students to go to reputable Web sites just as you would encourage them to find accurate information in the library. Anyone can post a Web page whether the knowledge is factual or not. Although most Web sites try to maintain information integrity, some Web sites may not be accurate. Sites which have a domain of government (.gov), education (.edu), or organization (.org) should have factual information.

CHECK WEB SITES BEFORE USING THEM IN THE CLASSROOM

It is wise to check out all Web sites before allowing students to go online. Web site addresses change, move, and some sites might incorporate information not appropriate for young students. If by chance the address has changed and will no longer work, try using a search engine (pages 73–74) to find the new URL.

USING THE INTERNET WITHOUT BEING ONLINE

If you have used the Internet in your classroom, you probably have heard your students say, "It's too slow." Or maybe you have said, "There is too much information out there." Both of these are common complaints by teachers and students using the Internet. A software program called *Web Buddy* has been developed to remedy these problems. This program allows you to download an entire Web site onto the hard drive, a floppy disc, or a zip drive and then use the Web site later without being connected to the Internet. This enables you to do extraordinary lessons in the classroom while accessing Web information at high speed without the fear of students accessing needless or inappropriate Web pages. One can also use *Web Buddy* to convert Web pages into word processing documents for you to edit and print. This is perfect for making classroom handouts!

When you or your students use these sites which have been transferred from *Web Buddy*, there is no need to actually be "on the Net." Thus, if you have the Internet at home or in the computer lab but not in your own classroom, *Web Buddy* would be ideal for you. The software and instruction manual are available by calling *Teacher Created Materials* at (800) 662-4321. The instruction manual entitled *Web Buddy*: Software, Instructions, & Projects is an excellent resource giving you step-by-step directions and many different uses for *Web Buddy*.

INTERNET ACTIVITIES FOR THE CLASSROOM

The next several pages are packed full of Internet activities to do in the classroom. These lessons are designed for the one-computer classroom. If you have projection capabilities such as a TV or large-screen projector, most of these lessons would be appropriate for you to do with the entire class. Other lessons would be more appropriate as a computer learning center where you rotate your students to the computer. This way, all the student are engaged in a meaningful project while you can keep a helpful eye on those working on the Internet. Eventually, all of the groups will have a turn to do this project.

Although this book only contains one chapter on the Internet, there are excellent books available that are dedicated entirely to Internet activities. These books which are published by Teacher Created Materials include *The Best of Internet Activities, Internet Activities for Math, Internet Activities for Science, Internet Activities for Social Studies,* and *Internet Activities for Language Arts.*

Once your students become proficient on the Internet, you may want to honor them with an Internet Wizard Certificate as shown below.

Congratulations!

This Award Is to Certify That

____

Is an Internet Wizard!

Signed: ______________________________

Date:______________

VIRTUAL FIELD TRIPS

Objective:

Would you like to take your students on more field trips, but your cost is limited and most of the places you would like to visit are too far away? Don't limit yourself or the curriculum any longer. Take your class on a virtual field trip instead.

Web Site Addresses:

Virtual Williamsburg	http://www.gc.net/wol/wol.html
White House	http://www.whitehouse.gov
Crayola Crayon	http://www.crayola.com/crayola
Hands-On Children's Museum	http://www.hocm.org
Lego	http://www.lego.com
Grand Canyon	http://www.kaibab.org/grand.htm

Instructions:

- Choose the place you want students to visit. Consider using one of the Web sites listed above. If you want to find a topic not listed above, use a search engine to find a good Web site on your topic (see page 73 for how to use a search engine).
- Distribute the Field Trip Log on the next page to all students.
- Students will be finding five interesting facts about the place they are visiting. Discuss with students that these should be new facts that have not already been discussed in class.
- Rotate students in pairs to view the field trip site.
- Students should complete their Field Trip Logs.
- Once everyone has had a turn at the computer, discuss the Field Trip Logs as a class.

Extension Ideas:

- Make a bulletin board showcasing your field trip. Include their Trip Logs and have students find pictures, maps, or postcards to decorate the bulletin board.
- Consider having your students share their field trip with another class at your school. Students could dress like reporters and make paper microphones.
- Have students present short reports from the field trip and then videotape them. This would be an interesting thing to show at Open House to parents!

FIELD TRIP LOG

SITE NAME: ______________________________

Web Site Address: ______________________________

Fact #1: ______________________________

____

Fact #2: ______________________________

____

Fact #3: ______________________________

____

Fact #4: ______________________________

____

Fact #5: ______________________________

____

THE WEATHER CHANNEL

Objective:

Students will enjoy learning more about the weather in their city and comparing weather data with cities all over the world. This is an excellent lesson for intermediate students and would correlate well not only with a weather unit but also with a geography unit.

Web Site Address:

http://www.weather.com

Instructions:

- Distribute a copy of each of the next two pages to each student. Review it together to prepare for the investigation. If possible, demonstrate the first part of the lesson to the class.
- Students will launch the Weather Channel Web site.
- Students will type the name of their city or of a large city near their houses, and then click on GO CITY.
- The students will browse through the Web site to find the answers to the questions by using the up, down, back, and forward arrows.
- Students will find the current temperature and humidity in their city.
- Students will check to see which is the best day for a BBQ in the next week (this lesson would be more appropriate in warmer weather).
- Students will look at the Doppler radar to find any precipitation in their city.
- Students will look at the travel conditions in their city and check on flight delays across America.
- Students will visit international cities and compare temperatures.

Extension Ideas:

- The Weather Channel Web site is extremely comprehensive. The Health and Allergy section would be an excellent platform for discussing why people have allergies, how allergies are related to weather, and how to grow some mold in your classroom!
- Have students use the International Weather section to create a Trip Around the World. Students could use this Web site to decide how to pack, which days would be better for certain activities, learn about flight delays, and more.

THE WEATHER CHANNEL *(cont.)*

Launch This Web Site:

http://www.weather.com

Answer the following questions by navigating through this Web site.

Type the name of your city under "Enter a City" and click GO CITY.

1. What is the current temperature in your city? ______________
2. What is the present humidity in your city? ______________________ Do you consider this high or low? ______________
3. How many minutes ago was this information updated (the Weather Channel is in the Eastern time zone; think about what time zone you're in)? ______________
4. If you were planning an outdoor BBQ in the next five days, which day or days would be best according to the weather? ______________ or ______________

Click on Doppler Radar.

5. Is there any rain in the entire beige area? ______________
6. Do you think your city has a chance of getting rain in the next 24 hours according to the Doppler radar? ______________

Click on the BACK arrow. Find the current temperature for Orlando, Florida.

7. Is Orlando, Florida, warmer or cooler right now than your city? ______________ By how many degrees? ______________

Complete this table.

	Your City	Chicago	Phoenix	Boston
Tomorrow's High Temp				
Tomorrow's Low Temp				

THE WEATHER CHANNEL *(cont.)*

Click on HEALTH AND ALLERGIES on the left hand side. Study the tree pollen map and then find the grass pollen map.

8. According to the two maps, is your city experiencing a higher level of tree pollen or grass pollen?

 ____

9. Why do you think this is? ______________________________

Click on TRAVEL CONDITIONS on the left-hand side. Study the map.

10. If a city has a yellow dot by it, what does that mean? ____________________

 ____

11. Click on the Los Angeles dot. How many minutes of delay are the airlines currently experiencing at the airport? ______________________

12. Are there any airports in America reporting more than a 45-minute delay? __ If so, name one: ______________________________

13. Check on the American Airlines flights from Chicago to Washington, D.C. If you were flying this route today, how many minutes of delay should you anticipate? __________

Click on INTERNATIONAL CITIES on the left-hand side. Type PARIS, and then click on Paris, France.

14. According to the current temperatures, how many degrees cooler is Paris than Phoenix?

 ____

Complete this table with the forecasted high temperatures in these cities.

	Paris, France	Kiev, Ukraine	Calcutta, India	Your Choice
Tomorrow's High				

THE VIRTUAL TOUR OF THE HUMAN BODY

Objective:

The human body is a fascinating machine. At this Web site, students will investigate many parts of the body, including the brain, heart, digestive system, skeletal system, and common injuries. This would be an excellent lesson for any human body unit.

Web Site Address:

http://www.medtropolis.com/vbody

Instructions:

- Discuss with students the human body. Make sure students have a general understanding of the human body before starting this lesson.
- Students will see the four sections of the body (i.e., heart, digestive system, brain, and skeleton) at this Web site. Students will be navigating through these four sections to find the answers to the questions on the following pages.
- Distribute a copy of each of the next two pages to each student in the class. Demonstrate the beginning of this lesson, if possible.
- Divide students into pairs and rotate them to the computer in the next week.
- Once all students have finished this exercise, discuss the answers as a class. Consider assigning students to investigate more about sports injuries and preventative measures.

Extension Ideas:

- The human body is a fascinating subject. There are many other wonderful Web sites to explore, such as the following two:

  http://www.innerbody.com

  http://www.americanheart.org

- Teachers may want to combine graphing with the lesson. Have students take their resting heart rates and record them. Then have students run in place for one minute and then take their heart rates. Have students record the data and graph differences.
- Invite a doctor, nurse, or trainer to your classroom. Have the expert talk about ways children can be healthier. For homework, have each student write a paragraph on this topic or make a personal action plan.

THE VIRTUAL TOUR OF THE HUMAN BODY *(cont.)*

Launch This Web Site:

http://www.medtropolis.com/vbody

Answer the following questions by navigating through this Web site.

1. Click on the BRAIN subheading. Scan through the list of articles to find an interesting fact about the following:

   A. Headaches: ______________________________

   ____

   B. Parkinson's Disease: ______________________________

   ____

2. Go back to the main page by clicking on the **BACK** arrow. Click on the Digestive System. Scan through the list of articles. Find two facts about how diet and lifestyle are related to the digestive system.

   A. ______________________________

   ____

   B. ______________________________

   ____

3. Go back to the main page by clicking on the **BACK** arrow. Click on the heart. Scan through the list of articles. Name two risk factors that increase a person's chances of having a heart attack.

   A. ______________________________

   ____

   B. ______________________________

   ____

THE VIRTUAL TOUR OF THE HUMAN BODY *(cont.)*

4. Read the article about women and heart disease. How common is heart disease in women? Explain.

____

____

5. Go back to the main page by clicking on the **BACK** arrow. Click on the Skeletal System. Look at the pulldown menu which tells the location of many bones in the body. Write the location of the following bones.

mandible: ______________________

tibia: ______________________

occipital bone: ______________________

femur: ______________________

metacarpal bones: ______________________

humerus: ______________________

ulna: ______________________

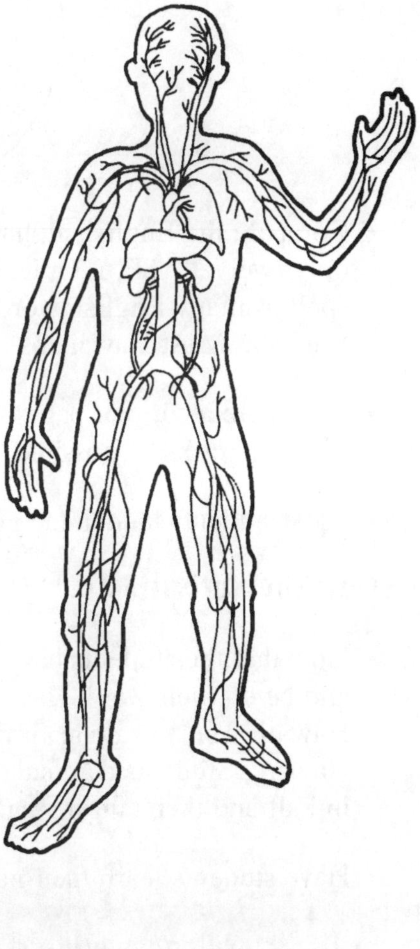

6. Click on the Sports Injuries article on this same page. Read this article to find two interesting facts about sports injuries.

A. ______________________

____

B. ______________________

____

HAWAII: THE LAND OF THE TROPICS

Objective:

A virtual trip to this tropical paradise is only a click away. Students will dream of visiting the real thing after learning about the Hawaiian Islands and the Hawaiian alphabet and language.

Web Site Address:

http://www.maui.net/~leodio/higuide.html

Instructions:

- Take a minute to compare and contrast Hawaii with your state. Draw a Venn diagram on the chalkboard to assist with this.

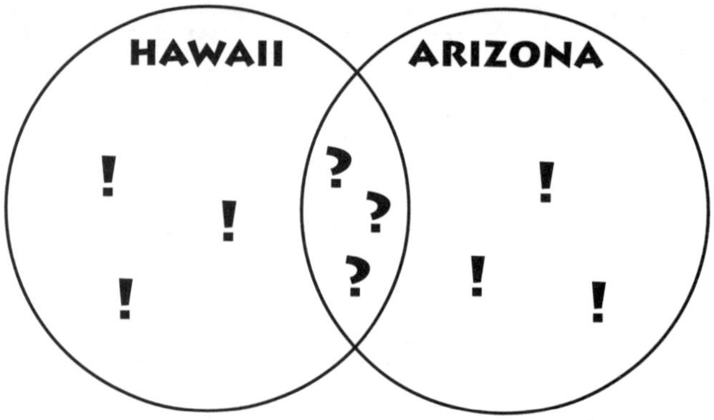

- Compare the English alphabet with twenty-six letters to that of the Hawaiian language which has only twelve: A, E, I, O, U, H, K, L, M, N, P, and W. Have students use these twelve letters to spell as many English words as possible. Explain that Hawaiian is a different language from English. Most Hawaiians speak English but also use their native language.
- Distribute a copy of page 87 to each student. Read over the directions in class and demonstrate the basic tasks, if possible.
- Have students launch the Hawaii Visitor Guide Web site and complete the activity page.

Extension Activities:

- Now that the students have visited the virtual Hawaii, they are probably ready to pack their bags and be on their way! Have students demonstrate what they learned by packing for a trip to Hawaii. Have students draw or cut out from a magazine pictures representing items to take to Hawaii. Students can make a simple suitcase by folding a 12" x 18" sheet of construction paper in half and then cutting handles.
- Have students learn their names in Hawaiian by launching this Web site:

  http://www.hisurf.com/cgi-bin/DM/hawaiian_name.cgi

Students can then make for their desks name tags showing their Hawaiian names. Have them decorate the name tags with pictures describing themselves.

HAWAII: THE LAND OF THE TROPICS *(cont.)*

Name____

Launch this Web site:

http://www.maui.net/~leodio/higuide.html

Follow the links to learn about Hawaii. Answer the questions.

Click the link called **Basics.**

1. How many islands are in the whole Hawaiian chain? ____________________________

2. What are the six principal islands of Hawaii?____________________________

3. If you were going to visit Hawaii, list four items you should take with you.

   ____

   ____

Click the arrow to go back. Then click the link **Glossary.**

4. Write the 12 letters that make up the Hawaiian alphabet.____________________________

   ____

5. Draw a line to match these Hawaiian and English words.

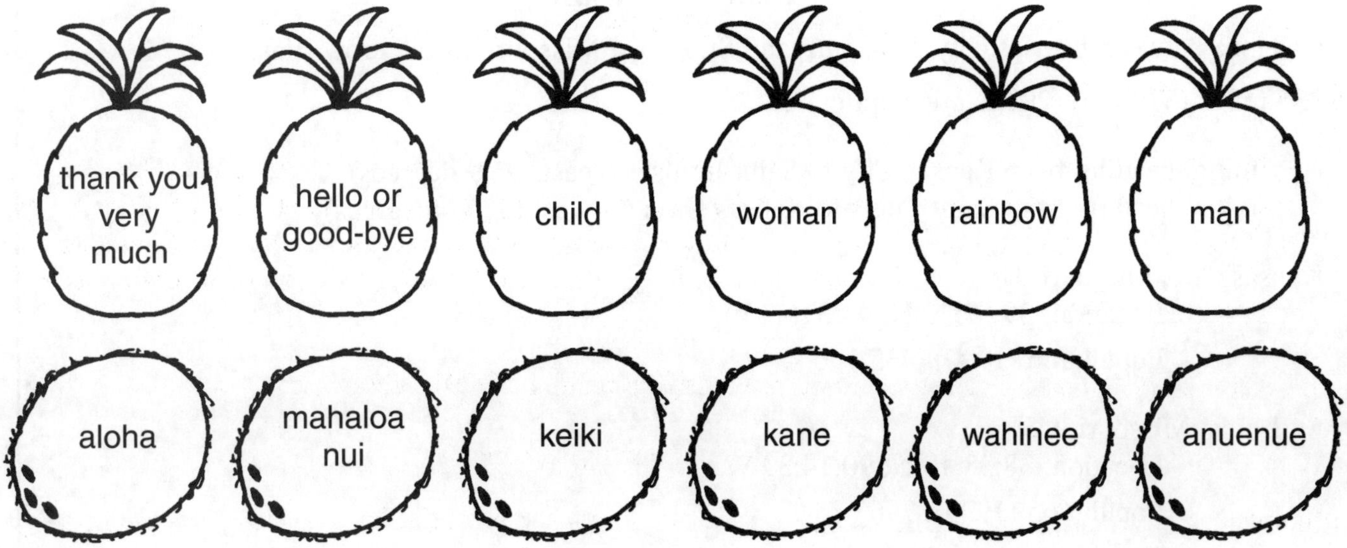

HOW FAR IS IT?

Objective:

Ever wanted to be able to find distances between cities or countries almost instantaneously? This is an excellent Web site to have bookmarked on your computer for quick access. This lesson will reinforce basic map skills.

Web Site Address:

http://www.indo.com/distance

Instructions:

- Have a class discussion about distance. Have students brainstorm to find three cities which are about 250 miles away from your city.
- Launch this Web site with the whole class. Type in the names of your city and the first of the three cities you chose from the brainstorming session.

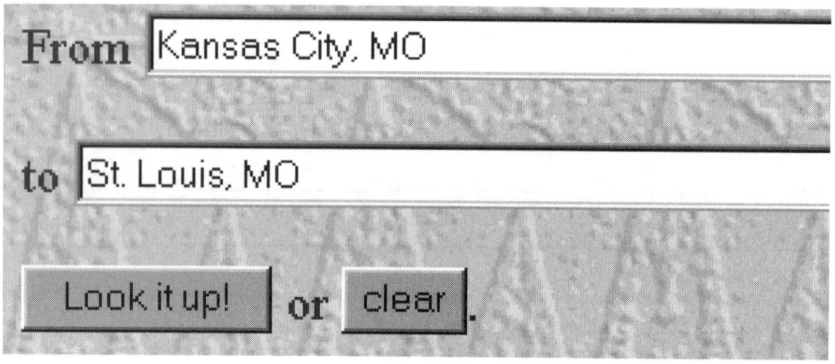

- Click on "LOOK IT UP!" and see if the students were correct. The result will look similar to the figure below.

Distance Result

Distance between Kansas City, Missouri, and St. Louis, Missouri, as the crow flies:

235 miles (378 km) (204 nautical miles)

Initial heading from Kansas City to Saint Louis: east (96.9 degrees)
Initial heading from Saint Louis to Kansas City: west (279.6 degrees)

Kansas City, Missouri, US
Location: 39:07:20 N, 94:33:07 W
Population (1990): 435,146

St. Louis, Missouri, US
Location: 38:38:10 N, 90:14:39 W
Population (1990): 396,685

HOW FAR IS IT? *(cont.)*

Instructions: *(cont.)*

- Continue this process until you have found three cities about 250 miles from your city.
- Print this information, if possible.
- Create some new distance questions for your students, such as the following:

  How far is it from your city to Disney World?

  Which is further from your state, Texas or Montana?

  What is the distance from your city to London, England?

  How many miles did a monarch butterfly migrate if it flew from your city to Mexico City?

Extension Ideas:

- Have students create math problems related to this Web site for their peers to solve. You could have your students write these problems on index cards and then post the cards near the computer.
- Create a trip starting and ending in your city that would be 900–1,000 miles. Visit three other cities. Students should find lodging and area attractions in each city. Have students go to Map Quest (http://www.mapquest.com) and find the exact driving directions for their trip.
- Copy a United States map for your students. Have them label your city. Have them mark five other cities on the map, all in different states. Using the "How Far Is It?" Web site, have students find the distances between the cities and your city and label their maps.
- Right before summer break, talk to students about places they are going to visit. Draw on the board a chart similar to the one below. Have students write under the appropriate heading the name of a city which they will be visiting during the break.

Places We Will Visit

Under 100 miles	Between 100–500 miles	Over 500 miles

THE TOP STORIES FROM USA TODAY

Objectives:

Current events will be forever part of the daily classroom. There are many newspapers and periodicals on the Internet available free to readers. Students will enjoy reading the *USA Today* newspaper online and learning about all of today's headlines.

Web Site Address:

http://www.usatoday.com

Instructions:

- Students will be launching the most recent *USA Today* from the Internet at http://www.usatoday.com.
- Bring a hard copy of today's *USA Today* paper. Show students the similarities between the hard copy and the Internet version. Show students the different sections of the newspaper at the top of the Web site (i.e., Sports, Money, Life, and Weather). Show students how these are the same sections in the hard copy of the newspaper.
- Copy and distribute the next page to your students.
- Put students in pairs or groups of three. Rotate students to the computer to complete this assignment.
- Once all the students are finished with this assignment, discuss the answers as a class.

Extension Ideas:

- Students may want to work in small groups and create a mini-newspaper of their own. Discuss with students the making of a newspaper, not only articles but headlines, pictures, etc.
- In addition to *USA Today,* there are many other newspapers and magazines online. Have students locate *Time Magazine* (http://www.time.com) and read about the cover story of the most recent issue. Students can also navigate through the Web site and find back issues of *Time.*

USATODAY.COM

Launch This Web Site:

http://www.usatoday.com

Answer the following questions by navigating through this Web site.

1. Date of newspaper: ______________________________

2. Top news headline of today: ______________________________

3. Read the lead article in the LIFE section and create a new headline for it: __________

   ____

4. Did the stock market go up or down? ______________________________

5. What is the major sports headline for today? ______________________________

6. Go to the weather section of *USA Today.* Name two states experiencing 50 degrees Fahrenheit (10 degrees Celsius) temperatures today. __________ & __________

7. Which U.S. regions are expecting precipitation today? ______________________________

8. Find an article which contains an opinion. What is the headline? __________

   ____

What is the opinion? ______________________________

____

____

9. On the front page of the *USA Today* paper, scroll down to the USA Snapshot. Explain this picture graph in your own words. ______________________________

   ____

10. Read an interesting article in this edition of *USA Today.* What is the headline?

    ____

Summarize the article in a few sentences. ______________________________

____

____

NATIVE AMERICANS

Objective:

The following pages feature activities related to four groups of Native Americans from different geographic regions of the United States: the Iroquois, the Pueblos tribes, Seminoles, and Sioux. Students access Web sites and gather information about these groups. Then they summarize their findings in an individual booklet.

Web Site Addresses:

Pueblo:	http://hanksville.phast.umass.edu/defs/independent/PCC/PCC.html#toc
Seminole:	http://www.seminoletribe.com
General Native American Sites:	http://www3.pitt.edu/~lmitten/indians.html

Instructions:

- On a United States map, show the students where Arizona and Florida are located. Briefly discuss these tribes and where they live.

  Seminoles—Florida   Pueblos—Arizona

- Each group will be making a four-page flip book highlighting each tribe. Pair students and assign them one of the groups listed above.
- Distribute the appropriate activity page to each student. Rotate pairs back to the computer to complete this activity page. Once students have gathered their information, they will be making a four-page flip book about their tribe. You may want students to work on this book as pairs or individually.

Making a Four-Page Flip Book

- Fold one sheet of pager 2 ½" (6.35 cm) from the top.
- Fold a second sheet of paper 4 ½" (11.43 cm) from the top.
- Place the second folded sheet inside the fold of the first.
- Staple in place.
- Write a title on the page.
- Write a detailed sentence at the bottom of each of three remaining pages about your tribe.
- Draw pictures to illustrate the text.

Name____

PUEBLOS OF THE SOUTHWEST

Launch this Web site:

http://hanksville.phast.umass.edu/defs/independent/PCC/PCC.html#toc

Read the information and answer the questions.

1. Circle the crafts at which the Pueblos are very good.

   pottery   puzzles   weaving   jewelry   leatherwork

2. Write three clans the Pueblos are divided into. ________________________________

   ____

3. Besides English, write one other language Pueblos speak. ______________________

4. Arrow down the page. Click on the link called **Pueblo Etiquette and Rules**. Read the information here and then list three things you should do and three things you should not do when visiting a Pueblo.

You should	**You should not**
______________________	______________________
______________________	______________________
______________________	______________________

5. Click the **Back** arrow to return to the home page. Then click on one of the nineteen Pueblo links. Write the name of the Pueblo and two interesting facts you learned about this community.

   ____

   ____

Name____

SEMINOLES

Launch this Web site:

http://www.seminoletribe.com/

Click the **Culture** link. Read the information to uncover the answers below (you will need to click the word links to find out more). Use the words from the word bank to fill in the blanks.

chickee	sweetgrass	Muscogee
sewing machine	turban	Miccosukee

These are two languages still spoken by Seminoles today: ____________ ____________

Baskets are made from ______________________________________.

A well-dressed Seminole man wears this on his head: ____________________________

This word means "house": ____________________________

This invention changed clothing styles beginning in 1900: ________________________

Circle five of the eight clans from the Seminole tribe.

Otter	Horse	Bear	Snake
Porcupine	Scorpion	Wind	Deer

OUR NATIONAL PARKS

Objectives:

- Becoming more confident on the Internet
- Scanning through information to find facts
- Drawing boxes and lines
- Typing facts in boxes and adjusting box size

Program Needed:

You will not only need access to the Internet but also a program in which you can paste clip art and draw boxes and lines. *Power Point* will work well for this project.

Instructions:

1. Find a blank map of the United States on a CD-ROM or another clip art program. Have the students copy and paste this map on the *Power Point* page.
2. Students should launch the Internet and find the national park service Web site at: **http://www.nps.gov**
3. Students should scan through this Web site and find facts on 4–7 national parks.
4. Students will also need to find the exact location of the national park (which is provided in this Web site).
5. Students will draw lines pointing to the location of each national park they have chosen. Students will attach a box to the line. In each box students will identify the park and write a fact about each.
6. Students will spell check their work and print.

Extension Ideas:

The study of national parks is great to do for a social studies unit. In addition to doing the map, students could find the distance between each park. Students can go the "How Far Is It" Web site at **http://www.indo.com/distance/**to find the distance between national parks. Teachers may want to expand this project and have students organize a trip including transportation, lodging, and attractions. It would be wise to assign a maximum number of miles traveled and a limit on budget. Students could then make a poster showing their travel route and include details about transportation, lodging, and attractions.

OUR NATIONAL PARKS

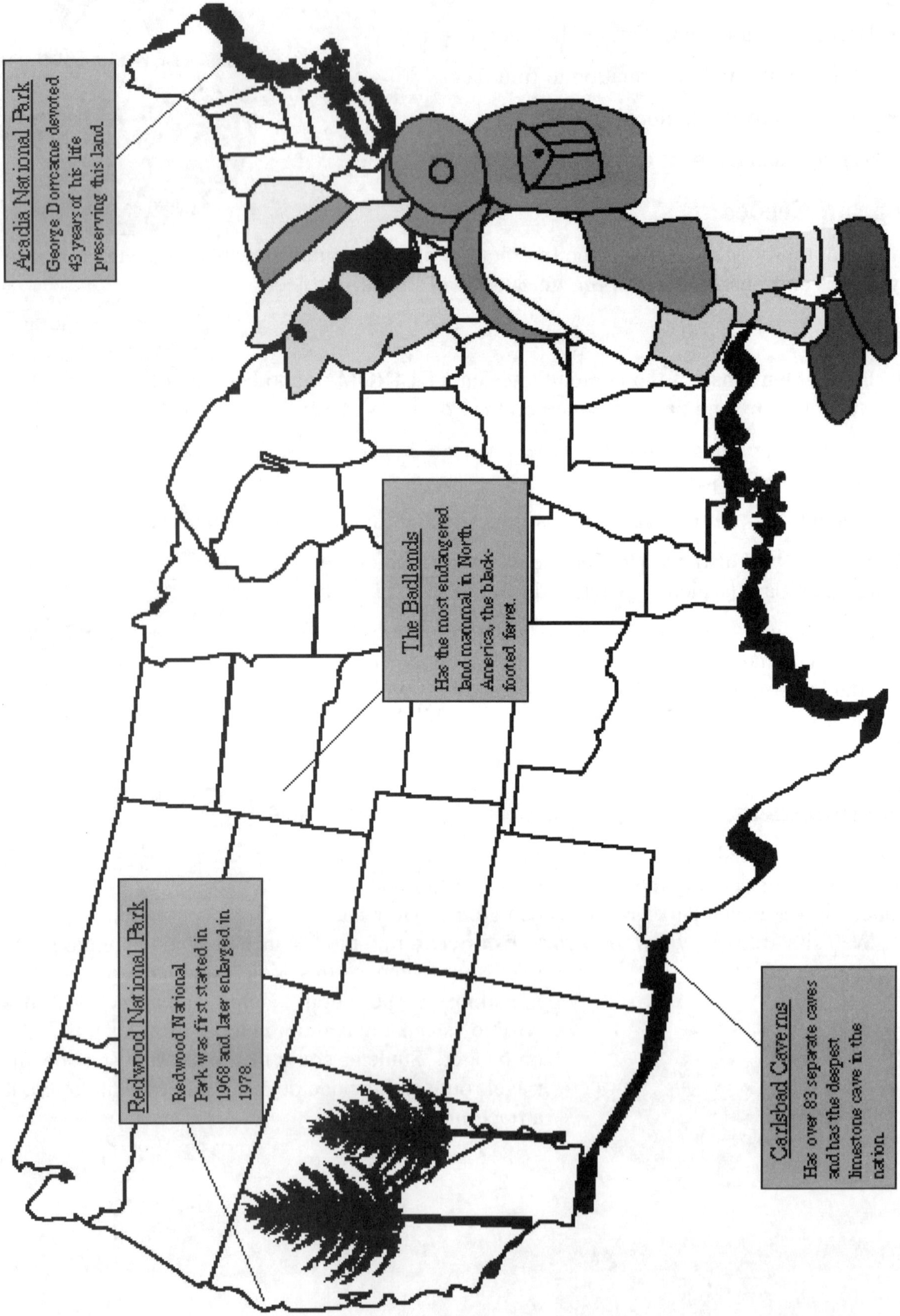

OTHER INTERNET WEB SITES

The Internet is full of interesting, educational Web sites which can enhance your curriculum. Although this book only contains one chapter on the Internet, there are excellent books available which are dedicated entirely to Internet activities. These books which are also published by Teacher Created Materials include *The Best of Internet Activities, Internet Activities for Math, Internet Activities for Social Studies, Internet Activities for Science,* and *Internet Activities for Language Arts.*

On the next few pages you will find resourceful Internet Web site addresses designed to get you started.

Language Arts Web Sites

Authors

Dr. Seuss
http://www.randomhouse.com/seussville/

Edgar Allan Poe
http://www.comnet.ca/~forrest/
http://www.poemuseum.org

Jan Brett
http://www.janbrett.com

Gary Paulsen
http://www.scils.rutgers.edu/special/kay/paulsen.html

Judy Blume
http://www.judyblume.com/home.html

Miscellaneous Language Arts Web Sites

Aesop's Fables
http://www.cruzio.com/~seaweb/corbin/aesop.html

Carol Hurst's Childrens Literature Site
http://www.carolhurst.com

Children's Literature Site
http://www.acs.ucalgary.ca/~dkbrown/

Fairy Tales and Folk Tales
http://darsie.ucdavis.edu/tales/

OTHER INTERNET WEB SITES *(cont.)*

LANGUAGE ARTS WEB SITES *(cont.)*

Miscellaneous Language Arts Web Sites *(cont.)*

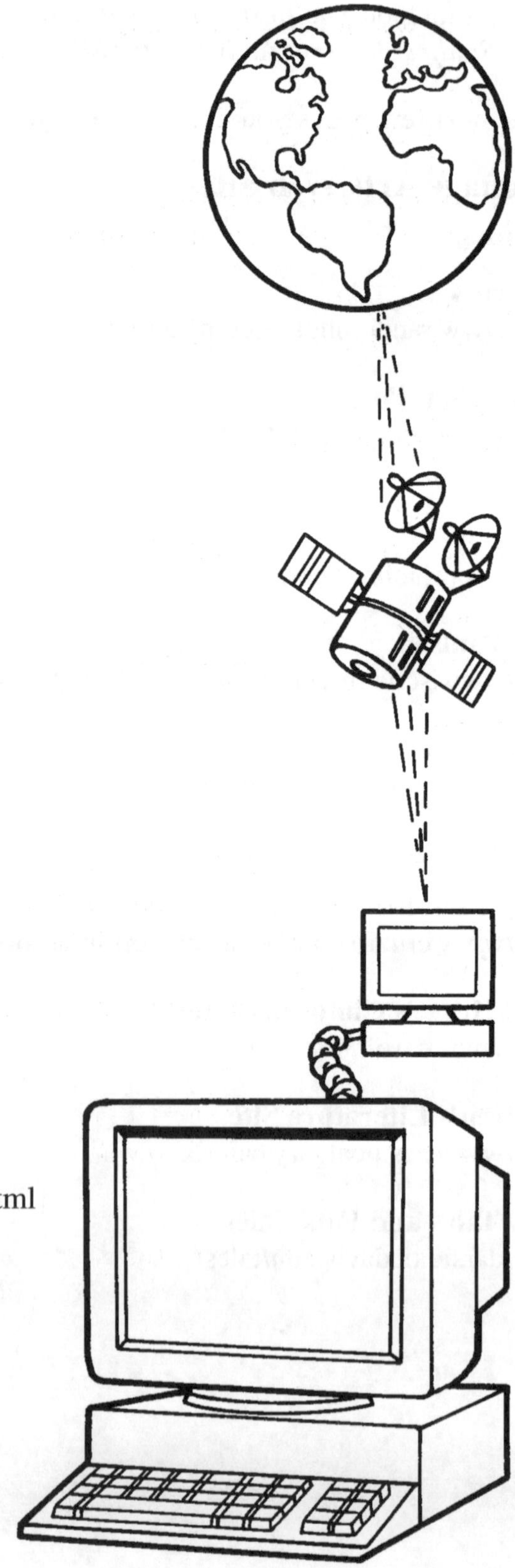

English as a Second Language
http://www.lang.uiuc.edu/r-li5/esl/

Guide to Grammar and Writing
http://cctc.commnet.edu/HP/pages/darling/grammar.htm
http://www.english.upenn.edu/~jlynch/grammar.html

Haiku Poetry
http://cc.matsuyama-u.ac.jp/~shiki/kim/kim.html
http://home.clara.net/pka/haiku/haiku.htm

Internet Public Library
http://www.ipl.org/youth/AskAuthor/

Magazines
http://www.enews.com

Internet Medieval Sourcebook
http://www.fordham.edu/halsall/sbook.html

Myths and Legends
http://pubpages.unh.edu/~cbsiren/myth.html

Quotations Page
http://www.starlingtech.com/quotes/about.html

Reading & Language Arts Center
http://www.eduplace.com/rdg/index.html

Shakespeare
http://www-tech.mit.edu/Shakespeare/works.html

Story Starters
http://www.geocities.com/Athens/1573/activities/story1.html

Young Writers
http://www.inkspot.com/young/

OTHER INTERNET WEB SITES *(cont.)*

MATH WEB SITES

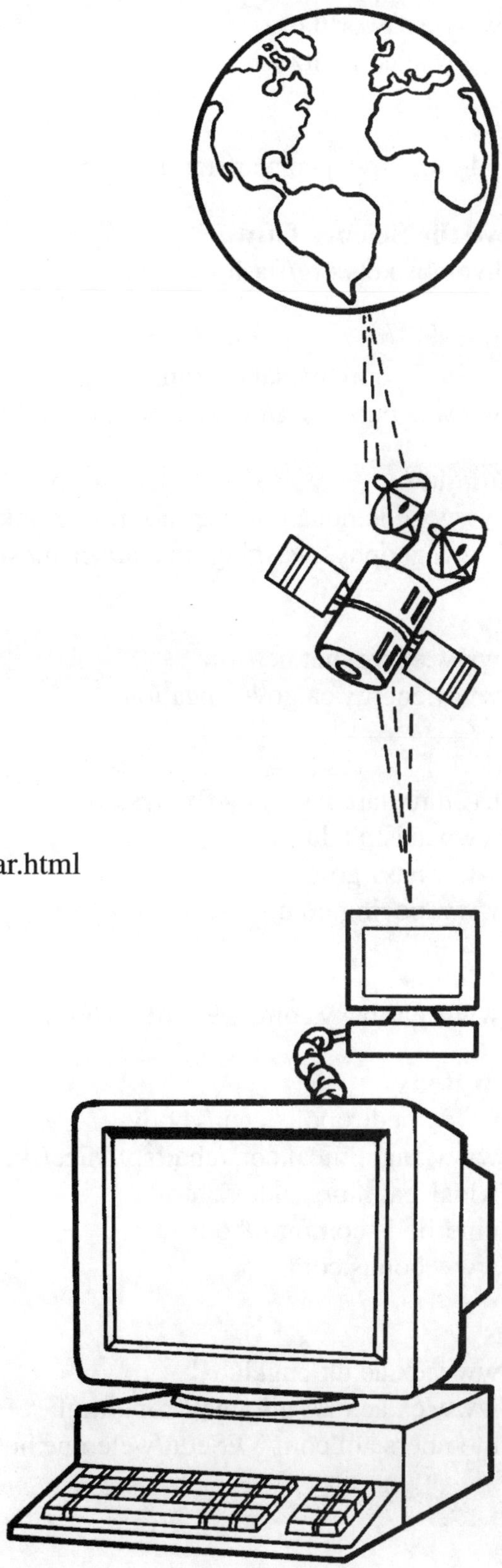

Ask Dr. Math
http://forum.swarthmore.edu/dr.math/

Dice Roll Server
http://www.irony.com/igroll.html

Elementary Problem of the Week
http://forum.swarthmore.edu/sum95/ruth/elem.pow.html

Flashcards for Kids
http://www.edu4kids.com/math/

Geometry Center
http://www.geom.umn.edu

Math Baseball
http://www.funbrain.com/math/index.html

Math Magic
http://forum.swarthmore.edu/mathmagic

Math Tables
http://www.sisweb.com/math/tables.htm

Mathematicians' Birthdays
http://www-groups.dcs.st-and.ac.uk/~history/Day_files/Year.html
http://dimacs.rutgers.edu/~judyann/calendar/Calendar.html

Mega Math
http://www.c3.lanl.gov/mega-math/welcome.html

Puzzles
http://alabanza.com/kabacoff/Inter-Links/
http://www.microtec.net~academy/mathpuzzle

Stock Market
http://www.ncsa.uiuc.edu/edu/RSE/RSEyellow/gnb.html

OTHER INTERNET WEB SITES *(cont.)*

SCIENCE WEB SITES

Animals
http://www.seaworld.org
http://www.si.edu/natzoo

Atoms
http://pdg.lbl.gov/cpep/startstandard.html

Bill Nye the Science Guy
http://nyelabs.kcts.org/flash_go.html

Dinosaurs
http://www.ZoomDinosaurs.com
http://www.acnatsci.org/dinosaurs/dinonew.html

Earthquakes
http://www.ngdc.noaa.gov/seg/hazard/earthqk.html
http://www.geophys.washington.edu/seismosurfing.html

Energy
http://www.energynet.net/
http://www.energy.ca.gov/education

Flight
http://k12unix.larc.nasa.gov/flyingstart/
http://www.nasm.edu
http://www.nasa.gov
http://www.boeing.com

Food Chains
http://www.earthsky.com/1996/es960406.html

Human Body
http://www.medtropolis.com/vbody
http://www.anatomical.com/chartsfullsize/skeletal.html
http://KidsHealth.org/index2.html
http://innerbody.com/htm/body.html
http://www.bonus.com

Insects
http://www.ex.ac.uk/bugclub
http://www.ex.ac.uk/~gjlramel/front.html
http://members.aol.com/YESedu/welcome.html/

OTHER INTERNET WEB SITES *(cont.)*

SCIENCE WEB SITES

Light
http://www.clp.berkeley.edu/CLP/CLP_Curriculum/light.html

Monarch Butterflies
http://www.monarchwatch.org
http://www.butterflywebsite.com

Night Creatures
http://www.torstar.com/rom/batcave/index.html
http://www.gorp.com/gorp/activity/wildlife/bats.htm

Oceans: Marine Life
http://www.redshift.com/~estarr/acs
http://www.whaletimes.org/whafshn.htm

Planets
http://www.seds.org/nineplanets/nineplanets/
http://www.hawastsoc.org/solar/
http://www.nasa.gov

Plants
http://www.fi.edu/tfi/units/life

Rain Forests
http://www.ran.org

Rocks and Minerals
http://www.rockhounds.com/rockshop/table.html

Roller Coaster in the Classroom: Potential and Kinetic Energy
http://www.col-ed.org/cur/sci/sci193.txt

Science Fair Information
http://www.minnetonka.k12.mn.us/support/science/tools/scifairs.html

Volcanoes
http://volcano.und.edu
http://vulcan.wr.usgs.gov
http://www.dartmouth.edu/~volcano

Weather
http://www.weather.com

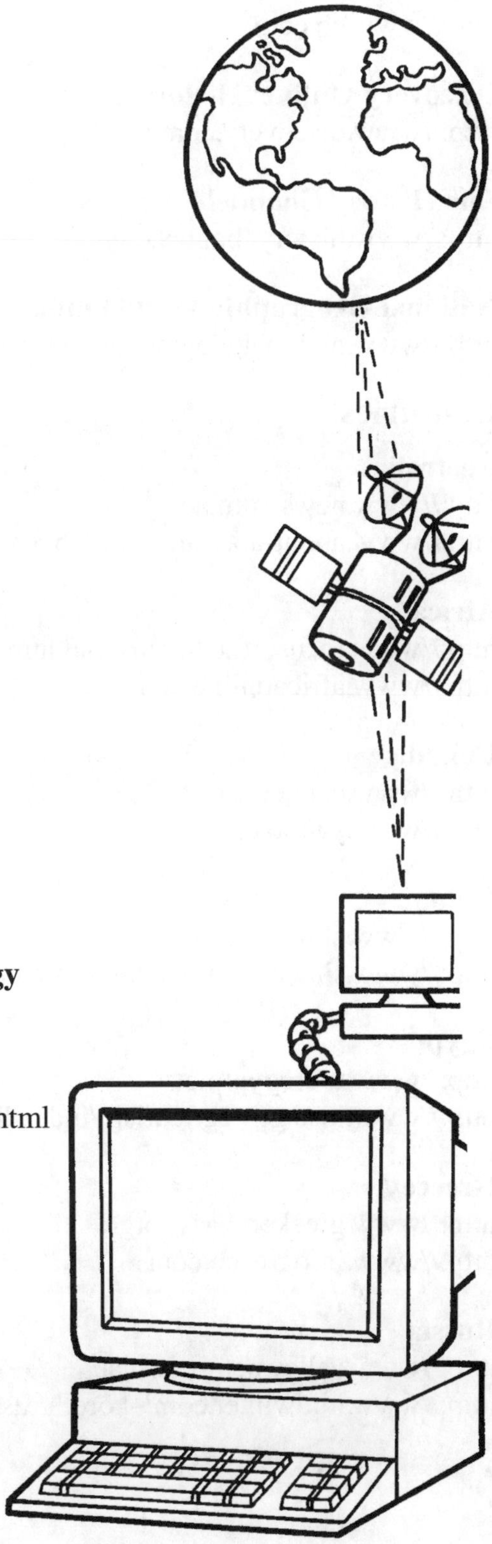

OTHER INTERNET WEB SITES (cont.)

SOCIAL STUDIES WEB SITES

General Social Studies

Britannica Online
http://www.eb.com

Discovery Online: History
http://www.discovery.com/past/stories/moretravels.html

The History Channel
http://www.historychannel.com

National Geographic World Online
http://www.nationalgeographic.com/media/world

Countries

Australia
http://www.news.com.au
http://www.about-australia.com/about.htm

Africa
http://www.focusintl.com/afriland.htm
http://www.africaonline.com

Canada
http://www.cangeo.ca
http://www.yahoo.ca

China
http://www.chinatoday.com
http://www.sinica.com/window-on-china/

Egypt
http://www.touregypt.net
http://www.idsc.gov.eg/tourism/index.htm

Greece
http://www.greekembassy.org/
http://www.infogreece.com

Russia
http://www.valley.net/~transnat/
http://www.midwinter.com/~koreth/russia

OTHER INTERNET WEB SITES *(cont.)*

SOCIAL STUDIES WEB SITES *(cont.)*

Famous People

Alexander Graham Bell
http://www.att.com:80/attlabs/brainspin/alexbell/

George Washington Carver
http://www.lib.lsu.edu/lib/chem/display/carver.html

Thomas Edison
http://edison-ford-estate.com/ed_bio.htm

Benjamin Franklin
http://sln.fi.edu/franklin/rotten.html
http://earlyamerica.com/lives/franklin/index.html

Wilbur and Orville Wright
http://www.hfmgv.org/histories/wright/wrights.html

Presidents of the United States
http://www.ipl.org/ref/POTUS
http://www.whitehouse.gov/WH/glimpse/presidents/html/presidents.html

Albert Einstein
http://www.geocities.com/CapeCanaveral/Lab/3555

Martin Luther King, Jr.
http://www.seattletimes.com/mlk/index.html
http://www.mecca.org/~crights/mlk.html

Jackie Robinson
http://www.utexas.edu/students/jackie

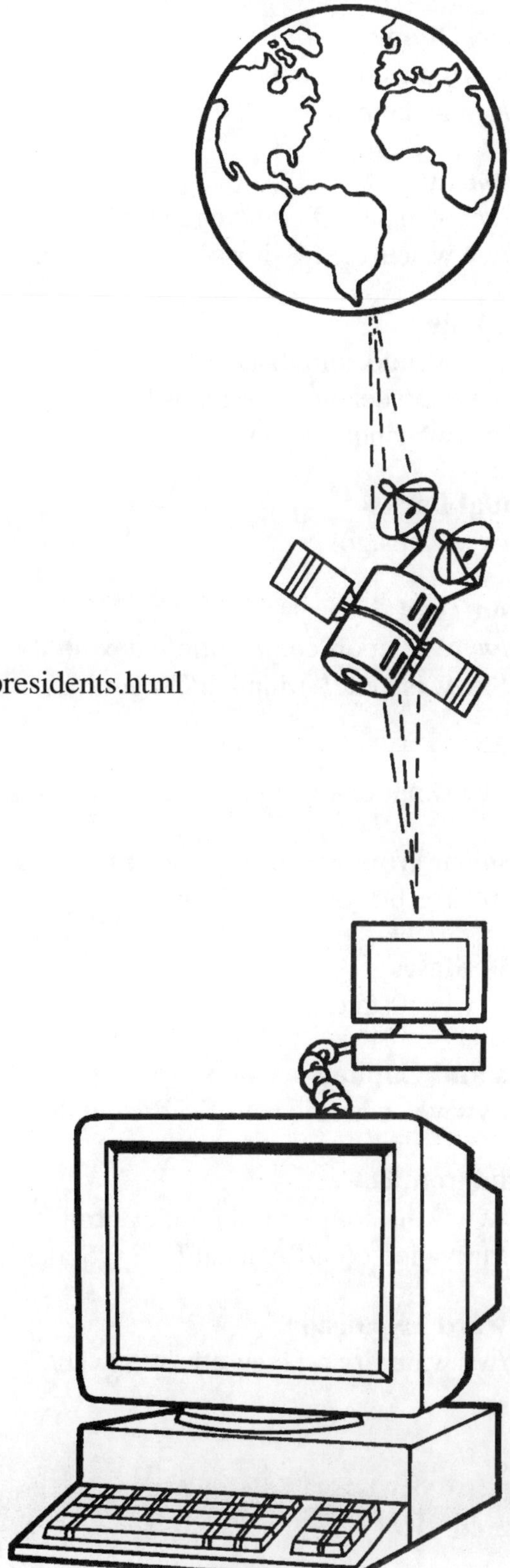

Imagination/Invention

U.S. Patent Process
http://www.patentspending.com

National Inventors Hall of Fame
http://www.invent.org/

Build It Yourself
http://northshore.shore.net/~biy/

OTHER INTERNET WEB SITES *(cont.)*

SOCIAL STUDIES WEB SITES *(cont.)*

Miscellaneous Social Studies Web Sites

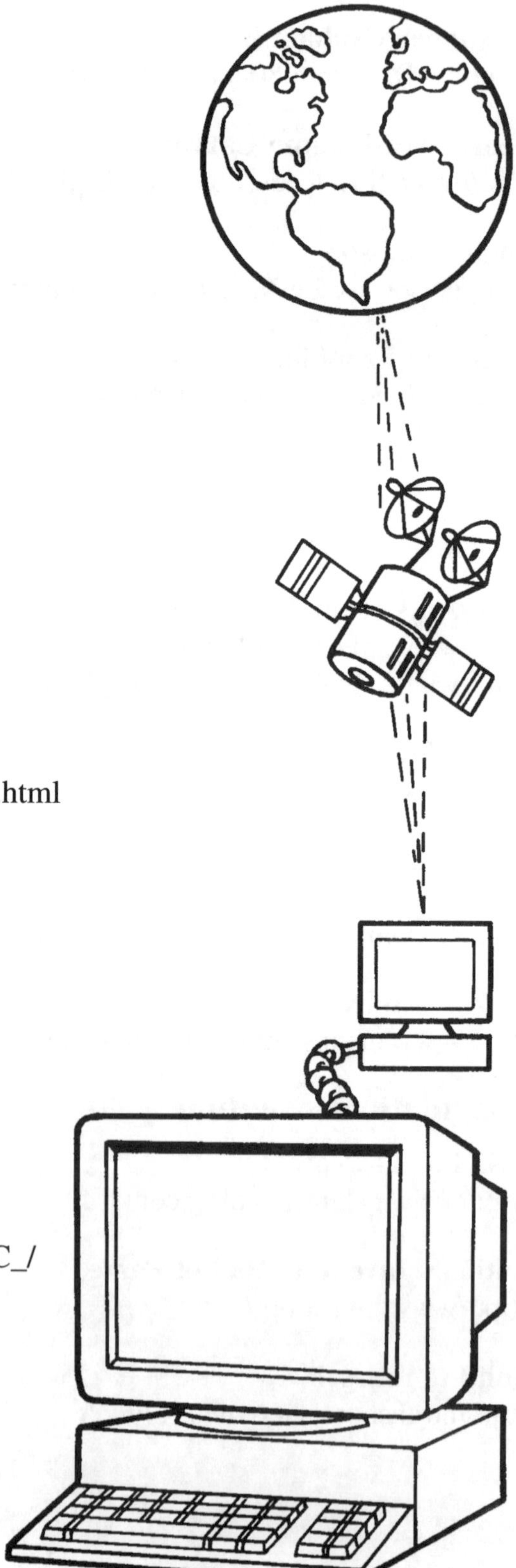

Ancient Olympics
http://olympics.tufts.edu/
http://orama.com/athens1896/

Gold Rush
http://www.malakoff.com/vcgc.htm
http://www.acusd.edu/~jross/goldrush.html

Map Skills
http://www.indo.com/distance
http://www.tradezone.com/maps.htm
http://www.mapquest.com

National Parks
http://www.nps.gov

Oregon Trail
http://www.teleport.com/~eotic/index.html
http://www.isu.edu/~trinmich/Oregontrail.html

Pirates
http://www.nationalgeographic.com/features/97/pirates/maina.html

The Seven Wonders of the Ancient World
http://pharos.bu.edu/Egypt/Wonders/

The 50 States
http://www.50states.com

States and Capitals
http://www.concentric.net/~Kraft/capitals/

Washington, D.C.
http://www.his.com/~matson/index.html
http://dir.yahoo.com/Regional/U_S__States/Washington__D_C_/

Westward Expansion
http://www.library.csi.cuny.edu/westweb/

OTHER INTERNET WEB SITES *(cont.)*

ART WEB SITES

Art Museums

Art Institute in Chicago
http://www.artic.edu/

Metropolitan Museum of Art
http://www.metmuseum.org

The Louvre
http://mistral.culture.fr/louvre

Smithsonian Institution
http://www.si.edu

Miscellaneous Art Sites

Coloring Book Pages
http://coloring.com/

Contests
http://www.artcontest.com

Mexican Art
http://www.cascade.net/kahlo.html
http://www.mexonline.com/culture.htm

Origami Art
http://www.jwindow.net/KIDS/SCHOOL/ART
http://www.the-village.com/origami/index.html

Photo Galleries

Bill Wright-Fine Art Photographer
http://www.wrightworld.com

Wildlife Photos
http://www.eaglestock.com/index.htm

OTHER INTERNET WEB SITES *(cont.)*

MUSIC WEB SITES

Classical Music
http://www.classical.net/music/composer/index.html
http://www.classical.net/music/links/musicgrp.html

Composers
http://members.aol.com/Orquesta/home.html

Database of Music Web Sites
http://discoveryschool.com/schrockguide/arts/artp.html

General Music Web Sites
http://orathost.cfa.ilstu.edu/public/KenFansler/onlinemusicpage.htm
http://www.billboard-online.com
http://www.geocities.com/Hollywood/Hills/5230/music2.html

Indianapolis Symphony Orchestra
http://www.in.net/iso

Music Education Online
http://www.geocities.com/Athens/2405/index.html

Musical Instruments
http://www.si.umich.edu/CHICO/MHN/enclpdia.html

Musical Instrument Puzzle Page
http://www.in.net/iso/ISOEDpg.html

Music World for Kids
http://members.aol.com/muswrld/

Resourcesfor Music Teachers
http://www.isd77.k12.MN.US/resources/staffpages/shirk/music.html

Sounds of Animals
http://www.georgetown.edu/cball/animals/animals.html

ELECTRONIC MAIL

Electronic mail or e-mail is the easiest and most common use of the Internet. Once you have an e-mail address, you will be able to send and receive correspondence with others on the Internet much like you do with regular postal mail. The difference between e-mail and postal mail (commonly called snail mail by e-mail users) is that it is delivered almost immediately. In addition, you can "enclose" or "attach" documents, files, or programs to the e-mail you are sending.

If you have your teacher-friend Bill Smith's Internet address (it might look like this: bsmith@aol.com), you can send him messages that will reach him almost instantly, even if he is in California and you are in Boston. For him to reply to you, normally he will simply need to click on "reply" and start typing. When he is through with his reply, it is a matter of another mouse click and off it goes.

Electronic mail can be really valuable within the school building or district, too. If the other teachers and administrators in your building have e-mail capabilities, then it is really easy to send them quick messages by using the computer without running down the hall. You may want to ask a fellow colleague "What time is the faculty meeting this afternoon?" or "Could I borrow the extra set of dictionaries for a lesson tomorrow?" Schools also may want to send their morning attendance or lunch counts to the front office via e-mail.

THE ANATOMY OF AN E-MAIL ADDRESS

E-mail addresses have three distinctive parts as shown in the diagram below.

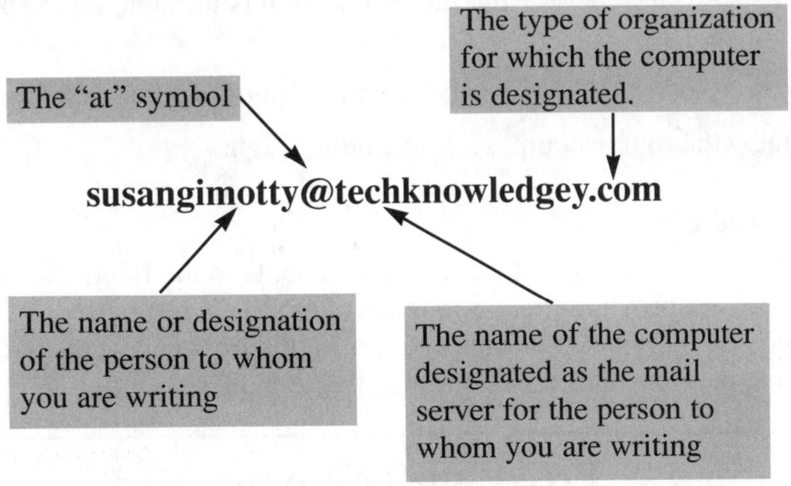

ELECTRONIC MAIL *(cont.)*

THE ANATOMY OF AN E-MAIL ADDRESS *(cont.)*

The suffix after the period will tell you what type of service is providing the e-mail account. A few of the more popular suffixes include the following:

Suffix	Type of Provider
.edu	Educational
.com	Commercial or business
.org	Nonprofit organization
.gov	Government
.mil	Military
.net	Network provider

WHERE DO YOU GET E-MAIL SOFTWARE?

If you have joined a commercial service such as America Online or CompuServe, your e-mail capability is built into its software. If your Internet connection is through a local provider, you will have two e-mail software choices:

- World Wide Web browsers such as Netscape Communicator or Microsoft Internet Explorer
- Software that came with your account, such as Eudora Light

FREE E-MAIL SOURCES

E-mail can be one of the easiest ways to introduce your students to the Internet. To help individuals get on the Internet, companies are providing free e-mail accounts. This is a perfect solution for the one-computer classroom because individual students could have their own accounts but all use the same computer. Below is a list of companies which provide free e-mail accounts.

Free E-mail Accounts

Juno	http://www.juno.com
Geocities	http://www.geocities.com
Hotmail	http://www.hotmail.com
NetAddress	http://www.netaddress.usa.net
Yahoo	http://mail.yahoo.com

ELECTRONIC MAIL *(cont.)*

HOW TO WRITE A MESSAGE

Writing an e-mail message is pretty simple. Here are the basic steps:

- Open your e-mail software program.
- Select a command called New Message.
- Type the recipient's e-mail address (such as bsmith@aol.com) where the e-mail form says "TO."
- Next, type your message's main theme (only a few words) next to: "SUBJECT."
- Click in the main message area and type your message.
- Finally, click the Send button. It will be a matter of minutes before the recipient receives your message.

ELECTRONIC MAIL *(cont.)*

TIPS FOR WRITING GOOD E-MAIL MESSAGES

Writing good e-mail messages is somewhat different from writing letters. E-mail messages are generally briefer and to the point.

Writing E-Mail in Style

- Write your message so that the receiver will be able to understand its meaning without having to guess.
- Use meaningful subject lines so that the receiver can quickly determine what the message is about. When pressed for time, readers need to know what they must read now and what they can read later. If you want a fairly immediate response, words like "a question for you" hardly evoke action. Instead, squeeze in your question, such as, "Can I borrow VCR?"
- Never use all capital letters in an e-mail message. This is equivalent to shouting.
- As with all writing, keep your audience in mind. Friends will be more tolerant of ramblings, while acquaintances will probably want you to get to the heart of the message as quickly as possible.
- Use short paragraphs. Try to keep messages under 25 lines.
- If you are replying to e-mail, remind the recipient the issue you are discussing. If you just reply "Yes" to a message, the recipient may not remember the question originally asked. A better response would be "Yes, we are leaving for the field trip tomorrow at 9:00 A.M."
- Use creative punctuation. Find replacements for gestures and intonation.

- Use smileys :)
- ***Put asterisks around sentences you wish to emphasize.***
- Use capital letters to EMPHASIZE.

:-)	Smiling Smiley	8-)	Smiley with glasses
;-)	Winking Smiley	:-P	Smiley with tongue out
:-(	Sad Smiley	:-@	Yelling Smiley
:-I	Neutral Smiley	|-O	Yawning Smiley
:->	Smart-aleck Smiley	:-D	Laughing Smiley
>:->	Devilish Smiley	:-O	Surprised Smiley

ELECTRONIC MAIL *(cont.)*

CLASSROOM USES OF E-MAIL

There are a number of curriculum-related activities that you can do with e-mail in your classroom. For instance, you can find answers to questions about academic subjects, research topics for class reports, or just get another person's perspective on a particular topic. For example, you could e-mail a national park or monument headquarters and ask for brochures to be sent to you and your students. In addition to learning about our own United States, you can explore and begin to appreciate difference in other societies, cultures, and countries.

One of the first things you as a teacher need to do is locate keypals or pen pals for your students. Personal connections made through e-mail can help your students broaden their viewpoints on any number of issues. A keypal activity is appropriate an as instructional activity if you want to

- connect students with an expert or mentor in a particular field.
- practice a foreign language or learn about another culture or geographic location.
- communicate information on relevant topics quickly.
- request information for reports.

Sources for such projects, as well as finding classes and individuals wishing to correspond with others, are listed below.

Pen Pal Connection
http://www.epals.com/kpi.html

E-Mail KeyPal Connection
http://www.comenius.com/keypal/index.html

Classroom Connect
http://www.classroom.net

This source also lists teachers seeking keypals for their students.

MAILING LISTS

The advent of e-mail has spawned an exchange of ideas via this tool called mailing lists or Listservs. Literally, there are thousands of mailing lists each on a specific topic. If you see one that interests you, then you can subscribe to it. Once you have subscribed, you will receive other members' messages and so will every other member—similar to a blanket mailing.

HOW DOES EVERYONE ON THE LIST GET THE SAME MESSAGE?

When you send a message, you do not send it to each member. Instead, you send it to a computer whose software (called listserv, list processor, or majordomo) passes it on to other members.

HOW MUCH MAIL SHOULD I EXPECT?

An active list can net you over fifty messages a day! However, if the subject interests you, many of those fifty messages could be meaningful for you. Keep in mind that reading messages, or even deciding to delete messages without reading them, takes time. So if the quantity becomes overwhelming, you may find it worthwhile to unsubscribe. Many people simply subscribe and then unsubscribe after getting a specific question answered.

HOW DO I SUBSCRIBE TO A MAILING LIST?

To subscribe to a mailing list from your own e-mail program, this is what to do:

- If you want to subscribe to KIDSPHERE, an international discussion about kids, then you would e-mail them at the following address:

  Kidsphere-request@vms.cis.pitt.edu

- In the body of the message, type the words:

  Subscribe KIDSPHERE John Doe

  Substitute your own first and last names for John Doe.

HOW DO I UNSUBSCRIBE TO A MAILING LIST?

To unsubscribe to a mailing list from your own e-mail program, this is what to do:

- If you want to unsubscribe to KIDSPHERE, then you would e-mail them at the following address:

  Kidsphere-request@vms.cis.pitt.edu

- In the body of the message, type the words:

  Unsubscribe KIDSPHERE John Doe

  Substitute your own first and last names for John Doe.

Many mailing lists offer specific instructions on how to subscribe and unsubscribe. Be sure to read the instructions carefully.

MAILING LISTS *(cont.)*

IS THE MAILING LIST MODERATED?

Some mailing lists are moderated and some are not. In a moderated mailing list, an administrator views all the e-mail and only forwards the acceptable ones to the list members. Frequently asked questions, or FAQs, are not forwarded to save list users valuable time. The FAQ for a mailing list is usually avaialable at a Web site or through e-mail by request. Other messages which the administrator feels have no value or are inappropriate for the audience will simply be deleted before it reaches the list members. Administrators will often send mail back to the originators who don't follow the rules of the list.

Unmoderated lists may be just as valuable, but can also waste a lot of time. Unmoderated lists tend to be self-governing. Members many times will correct other list users' conduct.

EDUCATION-RELATED MAILING LISTS

Here are a few education-related mailing lists you might consider.

CHATBACK—special education discussion, listserv@sjuvm.stjohns.edu

EDTECH—education and technology list, listserv@msu.ed

EKIDS—Electronic Kids Internet Server list, marjordomo@citybeach.wa.edu.us

KIDCAFE—kids' discussion group, listserv@vm1.nodak.edu

KIDSPHERE—international discussion about kids, kidsphere@vms.cis.pitt.edu

WWWEDU—The World Wide Web in Education, listproc@educom.unc.edu

MAKING YOUR OWN WEB PAGE

One of the most fantastic things about the World Wide Web is that it is a place where you as an individual can have a presence. In fact, many people are amazed at how easy it is to author and maintain your own home page on the Web. Classrooms, schools, districts, and parent groups do it all of the time. The Web page may be as simple as posting class announcements and homework. If you want to get more sophisticated, you may try to add pictures (scanned or digital camera) of class activities or display student work.

WHAT SOFTWARE DO I NEED?

For years, creating Web pages required a knowledge of a computer programming language called html. Learning html language can take an incredible amount of time. Today, many software publishers have created Web authoring programs almost as easy to use as a word processor. Using one of these authoring programs allows you to create a Web page quite simply without knowing the html language. The following is a list of user-friendly Web authoring programs.

Web Authoring Software

Software: *HomePage*
Company: Claris Corporation
Web Address: http://www.claris.com/products/

Software: *PageMill*
Company: Adobe Corporation
Web Address: http://www.adobe.com/

Software: *Netscape Navigator Gold*
Company: Netscape Communications Corporation
Web Address: http://home.netscape.com

Software: *Front Page*
Company: Microsoft
Web Address: http://www.microsoft.com

MAKING YOUR OWN WEB PAGE (cont.)

STEPS TO PLANNING A HOME PAGE

1. Make decisions about what you want the world to see. There are several examples of classroom Web pages at Web66 (http://web66.coled.umn.edu/). Some ideas follow:

    - About the teacher
    - About the class
    - Activities done during the year
    - Interactive projects
    - Home-school communication
    - Links to sites that enhance the curriculum

2. After viewing several examples, design your Web page on a piece of paper. Look at sites where free Web art is available. Remember to keep track of where you got the graphics from so you can give the artist credit on your page.
3. Type all of the text that will appear on your Web page on a word processor. This way you can easily edit and spell check the document.
4. Put your page together using Web creation software discussed on the previous page.
5. Announce your Web page to the world. Have a Web page unveiling party, send notes home, or announce it in the school newspaper.

WEB CREATION TUTORS

There are several places on the Web which will show you step-by-step diresctions to author a Web page. Here are a few:

Web66 Primer

http://www.ncsa.uiuc.edu/General/Internet/WWW/HTMLPrimer.html

Weave Your Web

http://www.msg.net/tutorial

WHAT IS COOPERATIVE LEARNING?

Of all the ways the teacher can use the one-computer classroom, using the computer as a cooperative learning tool is one of the best. This chapter is very important to me personally because cooperative learning software is really what got me excited about using technology in the classroom. A mix of media in the classroom can create an incredibly dynamic environment for cooperative learning. There is something wonderful about students working together in teams researching, collaborating, creating, and solving problems together. Tom Snyder Productions specializes in producing cooperative learning software.

Students working together is not a new concept; however, using the computer to help facilitate cooperative learning is a rather new notion. Group learning is not necessarily cooperative learning. The difference between group learning and cooperative learning is interdependence. The members of the cooperative group need each other in order to be successful. Thus, the domineering student needs the quiet student's input to facilitate a cooperative solution.

THE TEACHER IS THE FACILITATOR

Cooperative learning software requires the teacher to be the facilitator or a coach. The role of the teacher is essential in setting the pace of the lesson and guiding student learning. Cooperative learning software respects the knowledge and experience of the teacher. It is the teacher who is perceptive enough to identify student problems, react with care, and find a helpful solution. Teachers can help prepare students in the classroom for a society full of cooperative, group experiences.

GROUP-MAKING TIPS

Tom Snyder Productions suggests a few guidelines in forming groups.

Each team is composed of students whose performance levels range from low to high.

Among the many benefits of cooperative learning is the opportunity for faster students to enhance their understanding by explaining concepts to slower students and for the slower students to get reinforcement of these concepts along with peer support and acceptance.

The average performance level of all the teams in the class is about equal.

Students come to school with competitive spirits. Creating groups of equal average ability makes for a level playing field. No one group has an obvious advantage over another group.

Ethnicity, race, and gender are evenly distributed among teams.

The main reason for this distribution is to help break down ethnic, racial, and gender barriers and stereotypes. When students of diverse backgrounds work together, they begin to respect each other as individuals rather than as members of a particular group. They learn to appreciate each other's learning styles and strengths.

The ideal size of a cooperative group is four students.

Generally, if the groups are too big, individual students have less opportunity to participate. If the groups are too small, there is not enough diversity. Four is a good number.

GROUP RULES

If cooperative learning is unfamiliar to your students, you might want to set some ground rules for group behavior. This list could be posted on the walls for easy reference. Such a list of rules might include the following:

- Do not speak while others are speaking.
- Listen to what others have to say. Their ideas may influence what you think.
- Give everyone a chance. Sometimes the strangest idea may turn out to be the best.
- Let the majority rule in all conflicts. Use voting when necessary.
- Never take someone else's books or materials. Be patient and let others read and decipher information for themselves. They will then share it with the group.
- Do not hesitate to ask your teammates for help if you need it.

RECOMMENDED COOPERATIVE LEARNING SOFTWARE

Fizz & Martina's Math Adventures by Tom Snyder Productions

Grades 1–6

Fizz & Martina's Math Adventures is a series of elementary school CD-ROM titles that help students understand and apply important basic math concepts. At the heart of each title is an exciting animated adventure story starring Fizz and Martina, two curious and creative kids from the town of Blue Falls. Students solve the math problems that arise in *Fizz & Martina's Math Adventures* and practice a range of essential problem-solving skills. Students watch and listen for important information, identify relevant data, choose the appropriate arithmetic operations, and compute the answers. *Fizz & Martina's Math Adventures* uses a cooperative approach that requires discussion and the sharing of ideas among students.

Titles Available

There are three math adventures to choose from.

Buddies for Life

Grades 1–2

Fizz and Martina both love to explore, and the town of Blue Falls awaits them but so does a bully, Trump, and his dog, Butcher. Math topics covered include

- simple addition and subtraction.
- estimating quantities.

Blue Falls Elementary

Grades 3–4

Fizz and Martina think they know who broke the school's cherished statue of Pinky McGee. But while solving this mystery, Fizz must face some problems of his own at home and at school. Math topics covered include

- addition/subtraction with one- and two-digit numbers.
- multiplication with one-digit numbers.
- computational estimation.

Lights, Camera, Fractions!

Grades 5–6

Fizz and Martina have become Blue Falls' most famous mystery writers. With every passing week, their new cable-TV detective show becomes more popular, and with every passing minute they face more treachery from Mr. Minimood and Trump. Math topics covered include

- fraction concepts.
- computational estimation.

RECOMMENDED COOPERATIVE LEARNING SOFTWARE *(cont.)*

Fizz & Martina's Math Adventures by Tom Snyder Productions *(cont.)*

How Long Does It Take?

Typically, it takes five class periods to complete each *Fizz & Martina's Math Adventures* title, one class period for the intro activity and a full class period for each of the four episodes. Each episode involves two context-rich math problems in which students follow a sequence of activities. Each math adventure title also includes optional follow-up activities and homework to accompany each episode.

Basic Steps

- Watch and Listen

  Students, arranged in teams, watch and listen to the animated story. They record important numbers and information which will help them solve the math problem encountered.

- Write and Coach

  Team members work together to complete the three questions on the Team Questions work sheet. Students must solve the problem posed in the story, explain how they found this solution, and describe the consequences for specific characters.

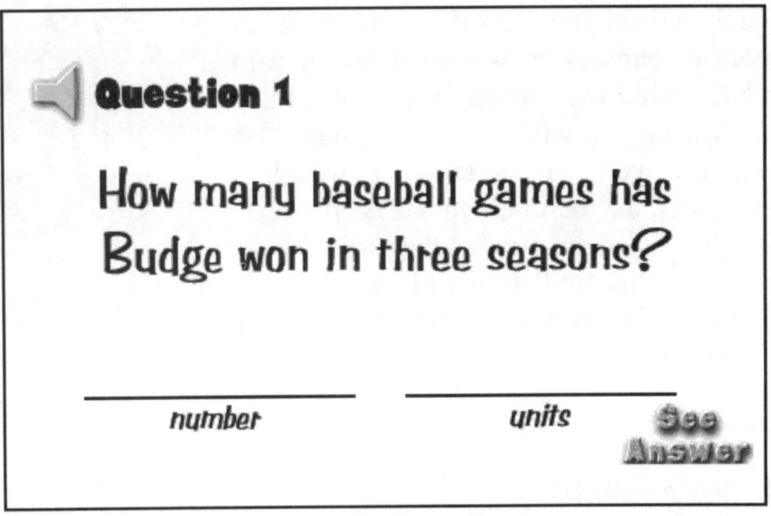

- Team Quiz

  For each question, the teacher picks a team and then chooses a student on the team to answer the question. The student must answer without looking at his or her written work. If a student's written and spoken answers are correct (based on the teacher's judgment), the teacher gives an "award card" to every student on that team, emphasizing that each member's contribution was important.

- Follow-up and Homework

  Optional follow-up activities reinforce and expand on the skills students have learned. Activities include the following:

- **Trivial Computes:** tests recall and provides additional computation practice.
- **The Estimation Game:** encourages students to use and explain computational estimation strategies.
- **Homework:** offers additional problem-solving practice.

RECOMMENDED COOPERATIVE LEARNING SOFTWARE *(cont.)*

Science Court by Tom Snyder Productions

Grades 4–6

Science Court is a CD-ROM series of several titles designed to teach students fundamental science concepts in elementary and middle school science. A humorous courtroom drama provides the vehicle for demonstrations and explanations as lawyers battle over a case. Courtroom correspondent Jen Betters is covering the trial. The students, working in cooperative teams, act as courtside commentators. At various breaks in the trial, Jen leads the students through a review of the facts, a hands-on activity, and a prediction about what will happen next. At the end of the trial, the students predict how the jury will vote.

How Long Does It Take?

Typically, it takes teachers two or three class periods to complete one *Science Court* title. There are four parts to the CD-ROM courtroom drama. At the end of parts 1, 2, and 3, you can do one or more hands-on activities. Students will then work in teams to answer six questions and predict what will happen next. Depending on how far you wish to carry the hands-on activities, you can expect to get through two parts, maybe three, in a class period. In part 4, students predict the jury's verdict. This prediction will take only part of a class period, unless students want to appeal.

Titles Available

There are twelve different *Science Court* CD-ROMs available. Topics include these:

- Electric Current
- Fossils
- Gravity
- Inertia
- Living Things
- Particles in Motion
- Seasons
- Soil
- Sound
- Statistics
- Water Cycle
- Work and Simple Machines

RECOMMENDED COOPERATIVE LEARNING SOFTWARE *(cont.)*

Science Court by Tom Snyder Productions *(cont.)*

Student Objectives

With *Science Court*, students will

- analyze and discuss scientific concepts.
- perform hands-on experiments.
- overcome common misconceptions in science.
- work cooperatively in groups.

Basic Steps

- Get organized. Put students in teams.

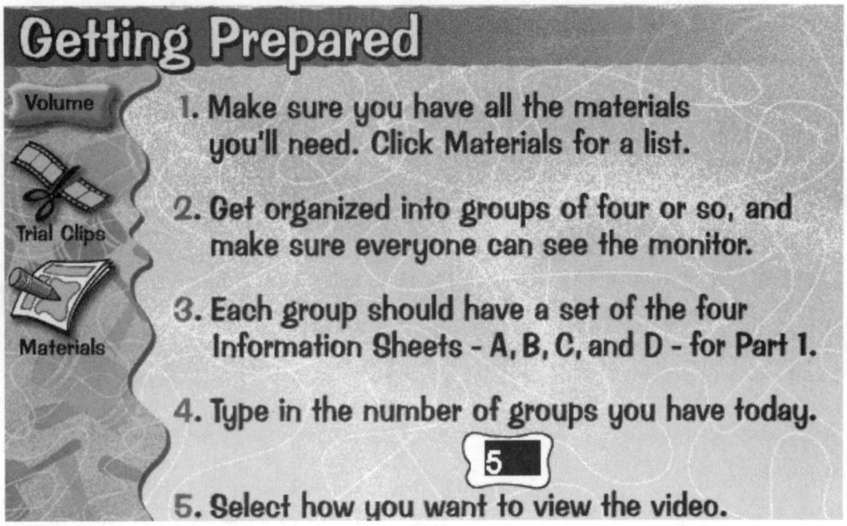

- Watch the video for part 1 of the trial (on the CD-ROM).

RECOMMENDED COOPERATIVE LEARNING SOFTWARE *(cont.)*

Science Court by Tom Snyder Productions *(cont.)*

Basic Steps *(cont.)*

- Answer questions.

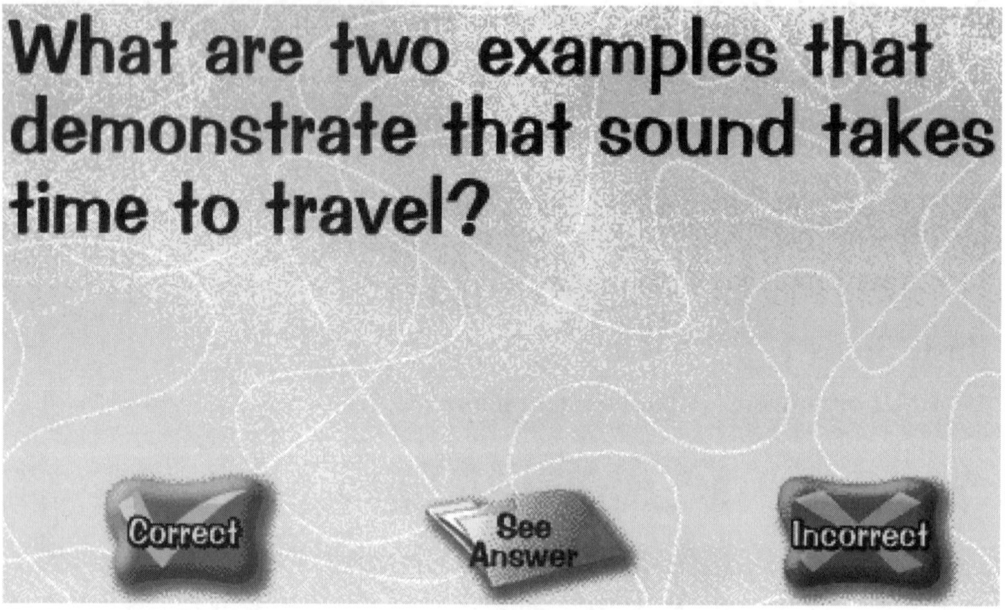

- Make a prediction as a class.

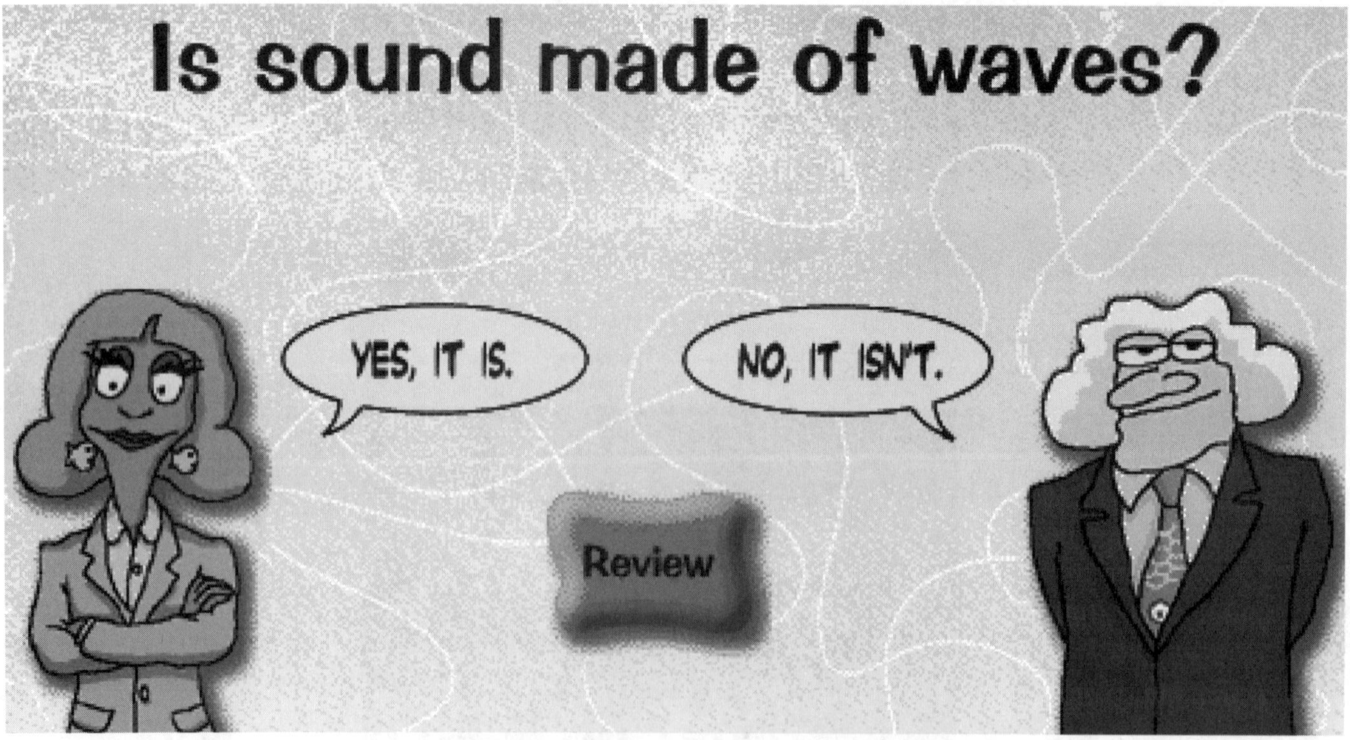

- *Complete all of the other parts of the trial.*
- *Predict a verdict.*

RECOMMENDED COOPERATIVE LEARNING SOFTWARE *(cont.)*

Science Court by Tom Snyder Productions *(cont.)*

Management

As with any cooperative learning activity, some students or teams will want to dominate the whole class. Tom Snyder Productions has included a Random Student/Team Picker in the software which allows the computer to randomly select a team or student to answer a question. Use the Random Picker as much as you want to solicit answers from as many students or teams as you want. You are in charge.

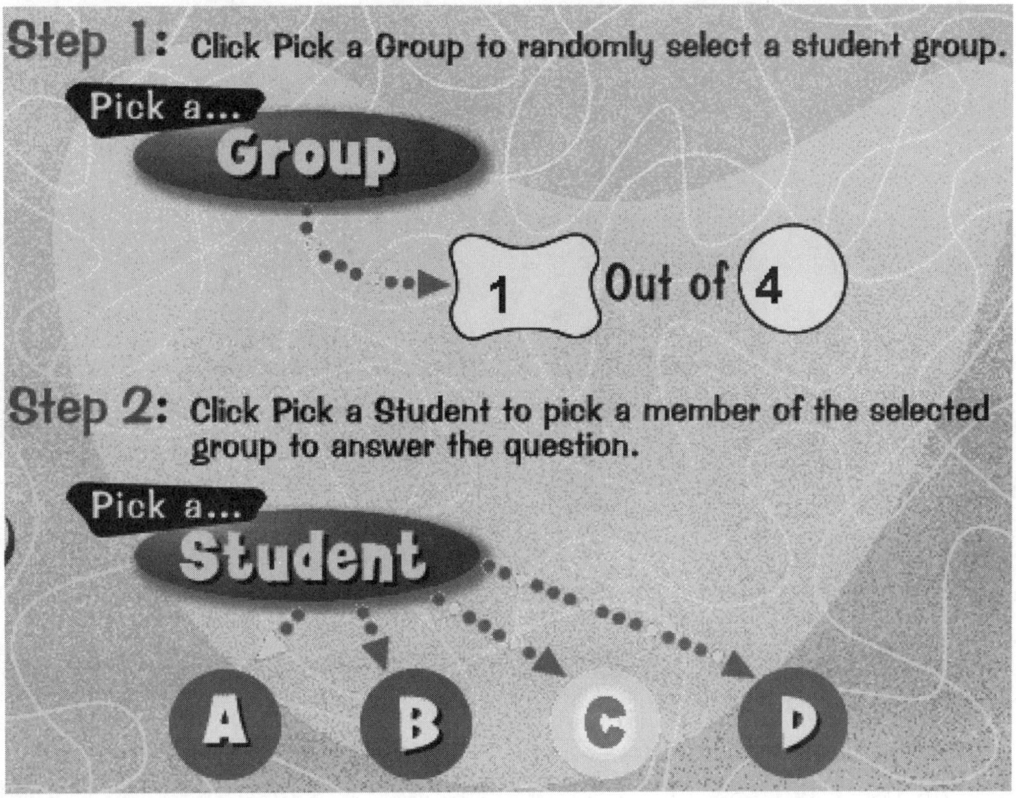

Assessment

There are a number of ways to assess what the students have learned by participating in a *Science Court* episode. In general, two main areas of learning are emphasized: retention of information and application of nnowledge.

Knowledge Retention

Each teacher's guide includes a test or quiz which corresponds to the CD-ROM. This assesses how well the students remembered basic concepts and vocabulary.

Application of Knowledge

Science Court also requires students to develop and use analytical skills. To assess these skills, the teacher's guide includes a test or quiz which presents students with a situation from daily life that involves the concepts presented on the CD-ROM.

RECOMMENDED COOPERATIVE LEARNING SOFTWARE *(cont.)*

PrimeTime Math by Tom Snyder Productions

Grades 6–8

PrimeTime Math engages your class in dramatic stories about firefighting, police work, and emergency medicine. Students watch a dramatic story, record data, read, write, calculate, and cooperate to solve problems set up by the CD-ROM. Students learn to apply math in real situations and work in groups to solve individual and group questions about situations portrayed in the video.

Titles Available

There are three different *PrimeTime Math* titles available.

PrimeTime Math: Stakeout!

Detectives are investigating a rash of robberies at local comic bookstores. Math topics covered include

- mean values, percentages, and ranges.
- using statistics to establish patterns.
- tables, bar graphs, and frequency charts.

PrimeTime Math: Emergency!

A patient arrives at the hospital, and an emergency team goes in to action. Math topics covered include

- conversions of metric units and equivalents.
- medical measurements and rates.
- graphs of values over time

PrimeTime Math: Fire!

A team of firefighters is called to the scene of a dangerous building fire. Math topics covered include

- basic algebraic formulas and order of operations.
- firefighting measurements and rates.
- triangles and Pythagorean theorem.

RECOMMENDED COOPERATIVE LEARNING SOFTWARE *(cont.)*

PrimeTime Math by Tom Snyder Productions *(cont.)*

How Long Does It Take?

Typically it takes two to four class periods to move through each *PrimeTime Math* title. Each title unfolds in three dramatic acts. Acts one and two involve students in a problem-solving situation and take up to two class periods each. During the first two acts students follow a sequence of activities: learn the data to collect, watch the video (twice), work on math problems, share answers, and have a group review of the answers. Act three is a short video resolution to the drama.

Basic Steps

- Get organized. Put students in teams.
- Choose an act.
- Prepare for this act.
- Learn your assignments.
- Watch the video (twice).
- Go to work on individual questions and group questions (away from the computer).
- Complete the answer round.
- Break for homework. After students complete their work sheets in class, they watch the video for the homework commercial. The animated commercial sets up a new context for practicing the same math skills at home to reinforce and extend the class experience.

RECOMMENDED COOPERATIVE LEARNING SOFTWARE *(cont.)*

The Inspirer Series by Tom Snyder Productions

Grades 4–12

The Inspirer Series takes teams of students on a scavenger hunt to a variety of places such as the United States, Europe, Africa, or Asia, depending on the title purchased. This program really shines as a multi-team activity with one computer and a classroom full of students. The goal of each *Inspirer* title is to travel throughout a particular country or continent collecting resources and visiting areas with specific geographic characteristics. Working in teams, students interpret maps, share key information, and plan strategies.

How Does It Work?

- The class is divided into teams of four students. Each student is equipped with a unique map and essential information to share with team members.
- The computer presents each team with a task. For example, in *National Inspirer* team 5 may be ask to start in Texas and travel to states that are major producers of coal or corn and finish in a state with a large land area.
- Now the teacher steps back and watches the students dive in! It may get a little noisy, but it's productive noise. You will hear them say: "Where are the corn states?" or "My map shows most of the coal states in the northeast."

RECOMMENDED COOPERATIVE LEARNING SOFTWARE *(cont.)*

The Inspirer Series by Tom Snyder Productions *(cont.)*

How Long Does It Take?

Each title should take between one and three class periods, depending on how involved you want to become.

Titles Available

National Inspirer

- locational geography of the 50 states
- distribution of United States natural resources
- characteristics of states and regions

International Inspirer

- locational geography of 185 nations
- interpretation of maps and graphs
- group problem solving

Europe Inspirer

- new countries of Eastern Europe
- locational geography of 48 countries
- distribution of national resources

Africa Inspirer

- geographic characteristics of Africa
- locational and topographical geography
- update of Eritrea and Democratic Republic of Congo

Asia Inspirer

- new countries in Central Asia
- distribution of resources and transportation routes
- locational geography from Israel to Indonesia

American History Inspirer: Civil War

- developments leading up to the Civil War
- westward expansion
- industrial Revolution
- antislavery movement
- state history
- interpretation of historical maps

RECOMMENDED COOPERATIVE LEARNING SOFTWARE *(cont.)*

The Inspirer Series by Tom Snyder Productions *(cont.)*

Basic Steps

- Get organized.

Create student teams, prepare materials, arrange the classroom to facilitate cooperative learning, establish rules for behavior, distribute materials, and explain rules for the activity.

- Teams receive their trip assignments.

  For example, in *National Inspirer* students may be asked to begin in South Dakota and with ten moves find any states that are major producers of soybeans. For extra points, students may be asked to end their trip in a state with ten thousand square miles or smaller.

- Students plan a trip.

  Without using the computer, teams complete a travel log which they hope will help them accomplish their trip assignment. Students use several maps given to each team at the beginning of the activity.

- One team uses the computer.

  Once a team has planned their entire trip, then they may go to the computer to enter their route. Each team member has a job to do at the computer whether it be at the keyboard, mouse, or reading off the states listed in their travel log. Students will click the states they want, and a line will connect the two state capitals.

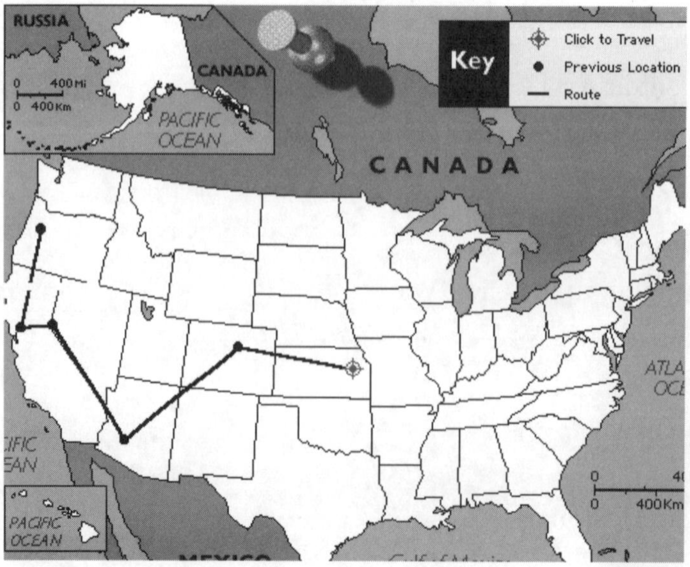

RECOMMENDED COOPERATIVE LEARNING SOFTWARE *(cont.)*

The Inspirer Series by Tom Snyder Productions *(cont.)*

Basic Steps *(cont.)*

- One team uses the computer. *(cont.)*
  If the team reaches a state that contains one of the resources they were asked to find, a bonus dialog box appears, showing the resources and the number of points earned.

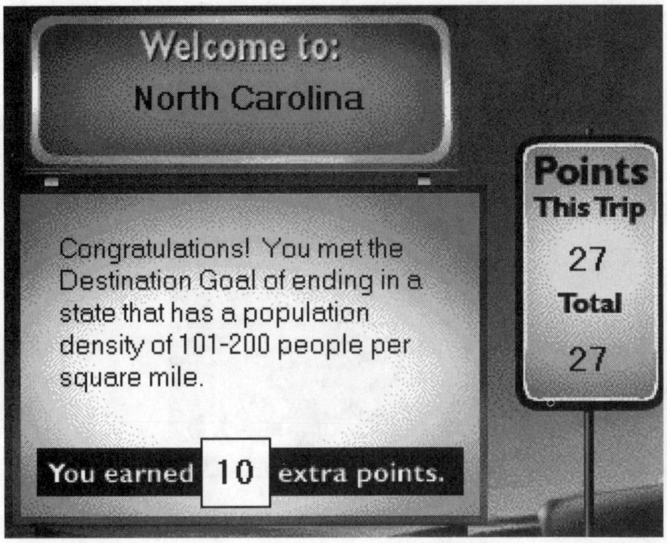

Once the team has made all ten moves, the computer will tell them how they have done. The computer will inform the team if they successfully reached their final destination state and give their total points.

Next, the team will be presented with a bonus question which is generally based on this trip. Students will have 20 seconds to answer. Usually, the answer can be found on one of the maps the team used to plan their trip.

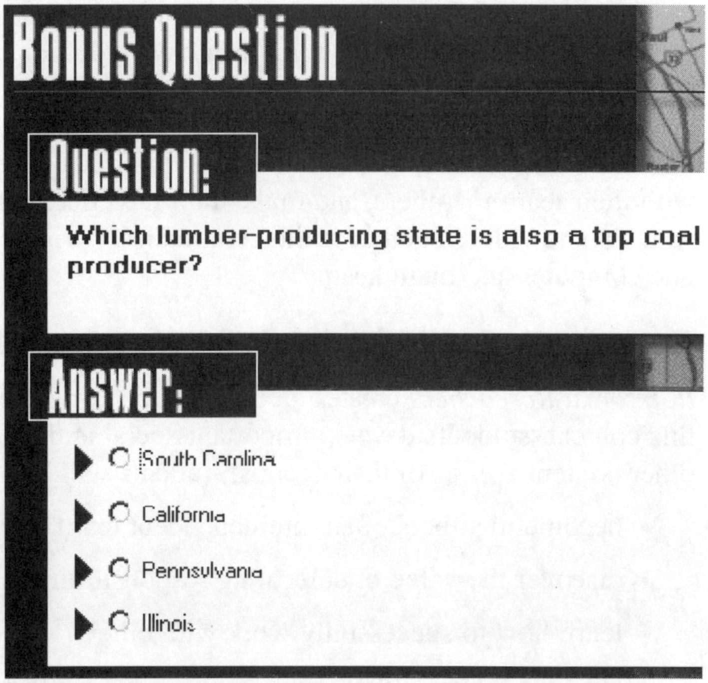

RECOMMENDED COOPERATIVE LEARNING SOFTWARE *(cont.)*

Rainforest Researchers by Tom Snyder Productions

Grades 5–8

Imagine your students in a remote Indonesian rain forest. With *Rainforest Researchers,* students become teams of scientists faced with two challenging assignments about rain forest plants. Each team consists of four members: a biologist, an ethnobotanist, a chemist, and an ecologist. As they probe the Indonesian rain forest for clues, teams explore the diverse and mysterious Web of life in this rich ecosystem. *Rainforest Researchers* provides a truly interactive experience that combines engaging scientific content with effective problem solving and critical thinking. *Rainforest Researchers* offers two realistic problems for students to solve: "The Case of the Disappearing Durians" and "The Search for the Lost Compound."

Using One Computer for Many Teams

Using *Rainforest Researchers* on one computer for an entire class allows you to keep all teams on the same step at the same time so you can closely facilitate team decision making. The software controls the pacing of multiple teams using the same program. Place the computer so that it is accessible by all teams on a rotating basis. Individual teams will go to the computer to enter their choices and get the information, and then they will return to their desks or tables to read their expert books, collaborate with their team members, and make their next decision. At a few points in the program, all teams may watch some video together at the computer. A printer is strongly recommended for success with the one computer and many teams.

Cooperative Learning Goals for *Rainforest Researchers*

Rainforest Reseachers creates a cooperative learning environment within a group of students. Within this context, students develop important social and leadership skills that they will carry with them into other content areas. In their groups, students will

- become members of an interdependent team.
- discover the value of delegating responsibility.
- learn how to successfully work with others.
- enhance their ability to communicate both information and opinions appropriately.

RECOMMENDED COOPERATIVE LEARNING SOFTWARE *(cont.)*

Rainforest Researchers by Tom Snyder Productions *(cont.)*

How to Use the Program

1. Divide the class into groups of four. Each scientific team includes a
    - biologist.
    - ethnobotanist.
    - chemist.
    - ecologist.
2. Watch the main intro video. Either the whole class watches the video or each team of four watches the video at the computer.
3. Teams read their books to understand their expert jobs and get prepared for the case.

After watching the case introductory video, teams then choose supplies necessary for the trip.

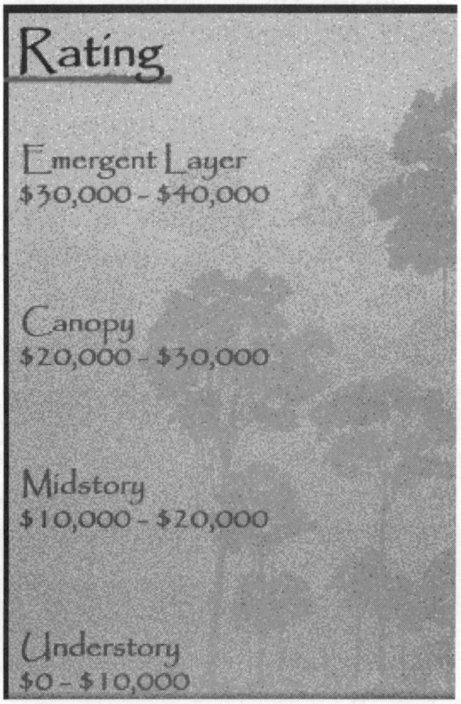

4. After watching more information about the case, students consult their books to choose an expert test. Teams visit the computer to see the results of their tests.
5. Using test results, surveys, and expert information in their books, teams rank the possible reasons for the problem and choose their solutions.
6. Teams gather around to see the outcome of the teams' efforts. Teams then see a report of where they stand financially and receive a researcher rating.

RECOMMENDED COOPERATIVE LEARNING SOFTWARE *(cont.)*

Rainforest Researchers by Tom Snyder Productions *(cont.)*

Each mission can take up to one or two weeks of class time, depending on your class size and how long you meet.

Extension Activities

Rainforest Researchers includes not only two main missions but also several extension activities. These activities require significantly less time than the main missions and are designed to expand learning. Some of the extension activities include

- "The Indonesian Traveler"
  Students pick a creative vehicle for learning and writing about the rainforests of Indonesia.
- "Nature's Pharmacy"
  Students research natural remedies in order to create a pharmacy filled with medicines derived from plants.
- "Stinky, but Yummy"
  Students investigate how different plants are used for food and spices in various cultures.
- "Products of the Rainforest"
  Students search for products that come from the rain forest to assess the ways that the forests can be used and sustained.

Hands-On Experiments

Rainforest Researchers also provides many hands-on experiments to extend the activity in your science curriculum. The experiments focus on plant biology and ecology. Some of the hands-on experiments include the following:

- "How Are Your Plants Different?"
  Students collect leaves and other plant parts, take photographs of the plants, and write detailed descriptions of the plants.
- "Fruit or Vegetable?"
  Students look at a variety of fruits and vegetable to understand the differences between scientific and common everyday terms.
- "Pollination"
  Students pollinate a flower and watch the development of seeds.
- "Making a Herbal First-Aid Kit"
  Using essential oils, students make a kit that includes recipes for insect repellent and for the treatment of sunburn, mosquito bites, and sore muscles.

OTHER SUGGESTED COOPERATIVE LEARNING SOFTWARE

To request a catalog for all of the Tom Snyder software listed in this section, call 1-800-342-0236 or visit their Web site at http://www.teachtsp.com.

Title: *El Niño*

Publisher: Tom Snyder Productions

Grade Level: 6–12

Working in teams, students role-play scientists who collect and interpret data in order to assess the El Niño effect. After developing a hypothesis, students test it by gathering and analyzing real NASA and NOAA data on sea surface temperatures, clouds, precipitation, currents, winds, and surface pressure.

Title: *Geography Search*

Publisher: Tom Snyder Productions

Grade Level: 5–9

Cooperative teams of students use the stars and the wind to navigate their way to the New World. Students learn how to use the stars and sun to determine latitude and longitude, study trade winds and the Earth's rotation, and understand global wind and weather patterns.

Title: *The Great Ocean Rescue*

Publisher: Tom Snyder Productions

Grade Level: 5–8

Turn your students into scientists who explore the world's oceans. Teams of students face four challenging rescue missions that take them deep into the world's oceans. To solve each problem, students must draw on information about ocean ecosystems, marine biology, Earth and environmental science, and a host of other subjects.

Title: *The Great Solar System Rescue*

Publisher: Tom Snyder Productions

Grade Level: 5–8

Cooperative teams of students must find and rescue probes lost in our solar system. Role-playing scientific experts, students use geology, planetary science, chemistry, and other subjects to guide their search. Students discover that teamwork and collaboration, as well as science, are the keys to success.

LEARNING TO DISCUSS

Another great use for the computer in the one-computer classroom is as a discussion generator. Students will meet people they disagree with throughout their lives. However, we cannot assume they will know how to negotiate with those people successfully. The universally valued skills of critical thinking and the ability to dialog, not just disagree, are not innate. These skills require constant and ongoing practice. Discussion-generating software is designed to assist you, the teacher, in teaching these valuable skills.

Discussion-generating software is designed to get a classroom of students engaged in a lively, informed discussion about a variety of topics from playground rules to ancient empires to prejudice. In addition to the software, each package comes with a class set of student reference books, teacher's guide, lesson plans, reproducibles, and a critical thinking supplement. The majority of the activity revolves around group discussions, reading printed material, role-playing, and student writing.

WHAT DOES THE COMPUTER DO?

Discussion-generating software does not focus on watching the computer only, but the computer does a host of other things such as

- acting as a resource by providing additional background.
- setting up scenarios.
- showing consequences for decisions.

WHAT DOES THE TEACHER DO?

The teacher's role is crucial in the success of discussion-generating software. The teacher's role includes

- acting as a facilitator for the activity.
- directing the discussion.
- pacing the activity.
- manipulating the computer.

RECOMMENDED DISCUSSION-GENERATING SOFTWARE

Choices, Choices by Tom Snyder Productions

Grades K–6

Young people face difficult choices every day, balancing their own values with the expectations of friends, parents, and teachers. *Choices, Choices* helps students develop the skills and awareness they need to make wise choices and to think through the consequences of their actions. This is a perfect activity for the one-computer classroom. Each title of *Choices, Choices* presents students with a challenging dilemma followed by choices for different ways to take action. At each decision-making point, the teacher leads the class in a dynamic discussion relating to various environmental and community-related issues. The computer presents the situation and provides consequences for each of the five decisions students must take. There are approximately 300 different paths students may take, and the same choices will not always lead to the same outcomes.

How Much Time Does It Take?

The length of time it takes to move through a *Choices, Choices* title will vary, depending on how you use the program. The whole package includes much more than computer software. The materials, along with the software, give teachers the tools to build a full unit on the topic, which could last a few days or a few weeks.

Creating a Curriculum

The materials included in a *Choices, Choices* title make it easy to build a unit, using the software as a foundation. The materials include a vocabulary section, lesson plans, and comic strip cards which all provide opportunities for you to extend the activity further into the curriculum.

RECOMMENDED DISCUSSION-GENERATING SOFTWARE *(cont.)*

Choices, Choices by Tom Snyder Productions *(cont.)*

The Basic Steps

- Understand the situation.

  Students are presented with a real-world dilemma via the computer. For example, it's time for soccer practice, but the field is covered with trash. What should they do?

- Set goals.

  Working together, students set goals. What is most important to them? Stress to students that there are not necessarily right or wrong answers, just different ideas.

RECOMMENDED DISCUSSION-GENERATING SOFTWARE *(cont.)*

Choices, Choices by Tom Snyder Productions *(cont.)*

The Basic Steps *(cont.)*

- Talk about your options.

Should they clean up the playground? Practice in spite of the mess? Whose responsibility is the trash? Students are encouraged to explain not just what they think but why they have particular opinions.

- Make a choice.

  Together, students make a decision and input their choice into the computer. Students should be reminded that, as in any democracy, sometimes people are not happy with what the majority decides. This is a good time to stress the value of thinking through the advantages and disadvantages of each choice.

- Think about the consequences.

  The computer shows the consequences, along with a new dilemma and new choices. After the final choice, students are given the opportunity to evaluate how completely they reached their goals. Students give themselves a thumbs-up (or down or sideways) to indicate how well they achieved their goals.

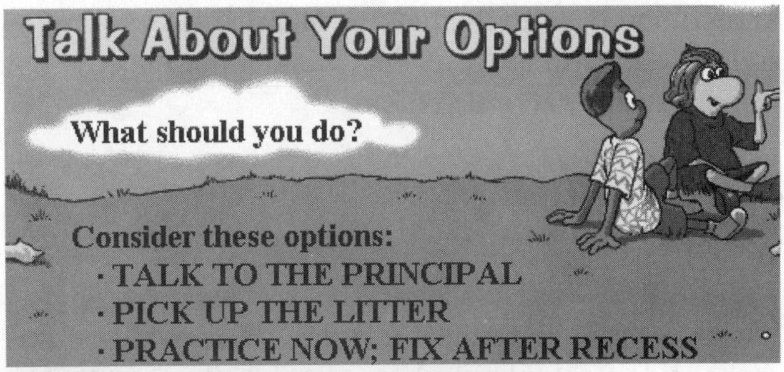

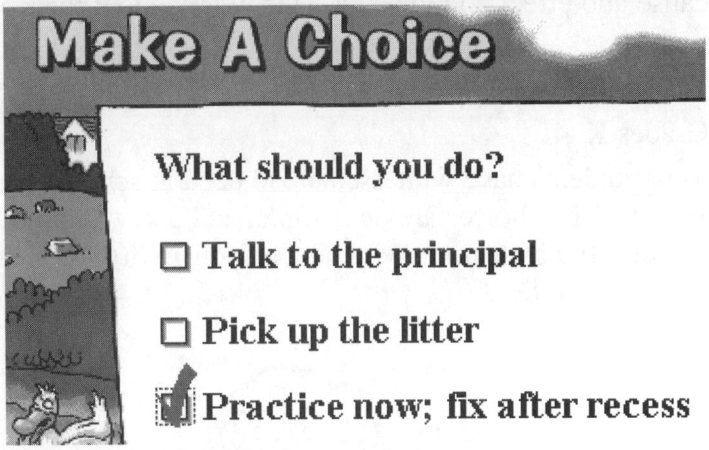

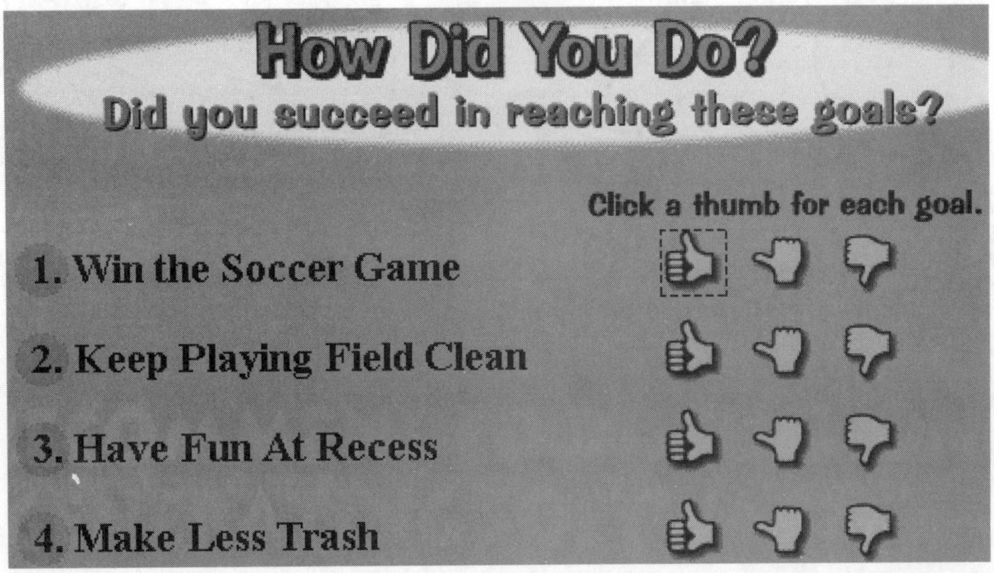

RECOMMENDED DISCUSSION-GENERATING SOFTWARE *(cont.)*

Choices, Choices by Tom Snyder Productions *(cont.)*

Titles Available

Kids and the Environment

Grades 2–6

It's recess time, and your soccer team needs to practice, but the playing field is covered with litter. Should you pick up the litter or practice anyway? How will your choices affect the team, the school, and the community? Students learn about the environment and discuss recycling, waste disposal, social responsibility, and much more.

On the Playground

Grades K–4

There is a new kid at school, and he does not seem to fit in. Will your students invite him to play ball? Which is more important—helping the new kid or pressure from peers to ignore him? Students learn cause and effect relationships as they talk about their behavior and the choices they make every day.

Taking Responsibility

Grades K–4

Your students have witnessed a bad deed at school. Do they tell the truth or choose not to tattle on their friend? The choices are not simple, and every action has its consequences. Students talk about issues of honesty and learn how to take responsibility for their behavior.

RECOMMENDED DISCUSSION-GENERATING SOFTWARE *(cont.)*

Decisions, Decisions by Tom Snyder Productions

Grades 5–10

With each title in the *Decisions, Decisions* series, students role-play a decision-maker faced with a critical situation drawn right from history, such as feudalism or a contemporary issue such as substance abuse. As presidents, feudal lords, mayors, or independence leaders, students use a proven five-step model for critical thinking and decision making to gather and review information, discuss options, and take action. Students not only acquire information but also learn how to use it.

Truly Interactive

Unlike other software, the *Decisions, Decisions* series is not designed for one or two students pushing buttons at a computer. Each *Decisions, Decisions* title sparks a thought-provoking, debate-rousing, thoroughly interactive experience in the classroom. And in this case, "interactive" means old-fashioned, human interaction. The best learning takes place when people interact with others: solving problems, sharing ideas, posing questions, and reaching for answers.

Discussing Sensitive Issues

Drinking and driving, prejudice, and substance abuse affect students at all levels and abilities, but not all classroom teachers are prepared to open up discussions about these issues. *Decisions, Decisions* titles designed to generate positive discussion about sensitive issues include *Substance Abuse, Prejudice, Violence in the Media, The Environment,* and *Lying, Cheating, and Stealing.* These *Decisions, Decisions* packages with their reference books and support activities address urgent issues for all students. Getting students to discuss constructively while developing decision-making skills will not by itself resolve these complicated issues, but it is a good start.

Why Bother with It?

After reading this lesson, you may ask yourself, "How is this so different from what I already do? If this lesson is really no different from what I already do, why bother using it?" The answer is efficiency and student motivation. It would be entirely possible to conduct this discussion using printed material only. By doing this, however, storage space becomes a major concern. With a file of student reference books and a small disk, all the information required for using the discussion-generating software is easily stored in a small area. Another advantage of using software is the neatness factor. Instead of having to flip back and forth through a binder or spread all the papers and options all over a table or chalkboard, the teacher selects a button on the computer and immediately brings up information. This is a much less frustrating and much more organized method of working through a program. And of course, student motivation is a great advantage, too. Students enjoy using the computer in virtually any capacity imaginable. Even though the bulk of this activity relies on student work instead of computer entertainment, most students believe that if they are using the computer even for a short period of time, work becomes fun. It is easy to see how the computer acts as an assistant to the teacher instead of taking center stage and running the show. Thus, curriculum is the engine; technology is but one of the tools.

RECOMMENDED DISCUSSION-GENERATING SOFTWARE *(cont.)*

Decisions, Decisions by Tom Snyder Productions *(cont.)*

The Basic Steps

- Analyze the situation.

  Students are presented with a real-world dilemma via the computer. Students must identify the main issues and separate fact from opinion.

- Determine goals.

  Students determine their long-term and short-term objectives for solving the problem. What is most important?

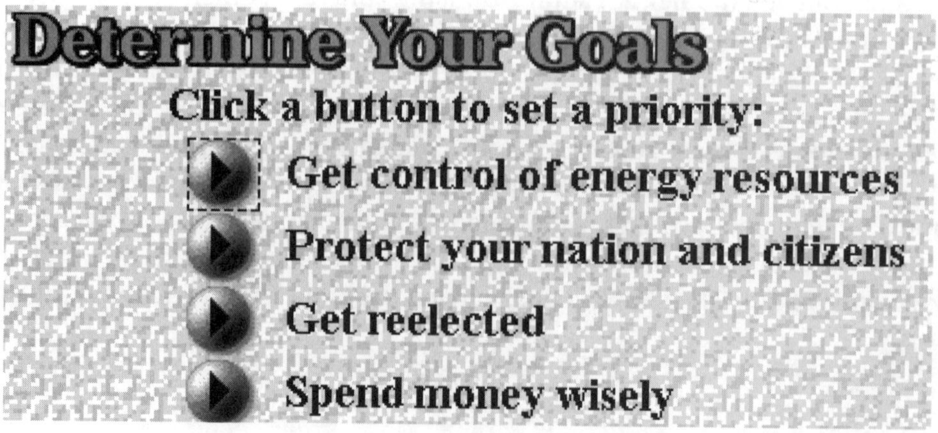

RECOMMENDED DISCUSSION-GENERATING SOFTWARE *(cont.)*

Decisions, Decisions by Tom Snyder Productions *(cont.)*

The Basic Steps *(cont.)*

- Consider your options.
  Opposing viewpoints and examples from history spark lively discussion as students reach a consensus about which action to take.

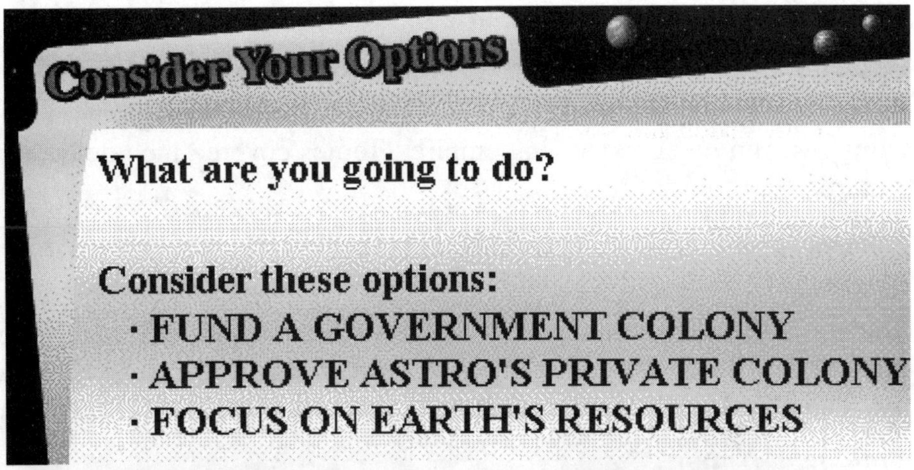

- Make a decision.
  Together, students make a decision and input their choice into the computer.

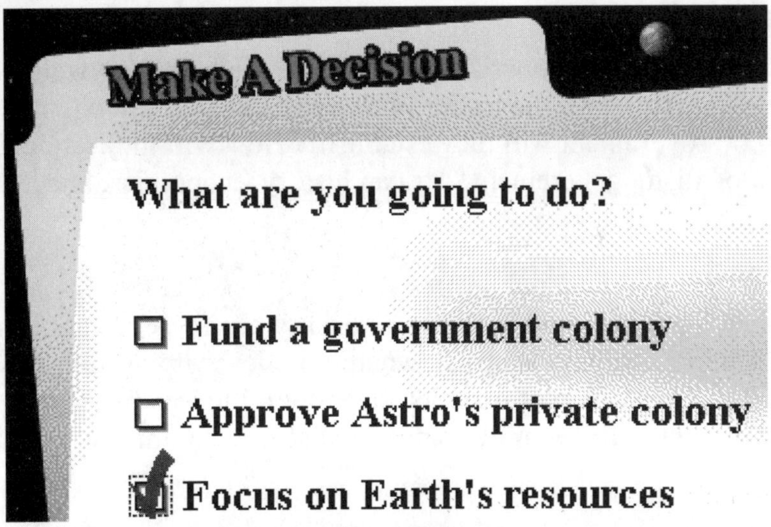

- Examine the consequences.
  The computer shows the decision's consequences. After the final decision, the teacher leads the class through a self-evaluation based on the goals they set at the beginning of the activity. The advisor reappears, and students are presented with new options to reconsider.

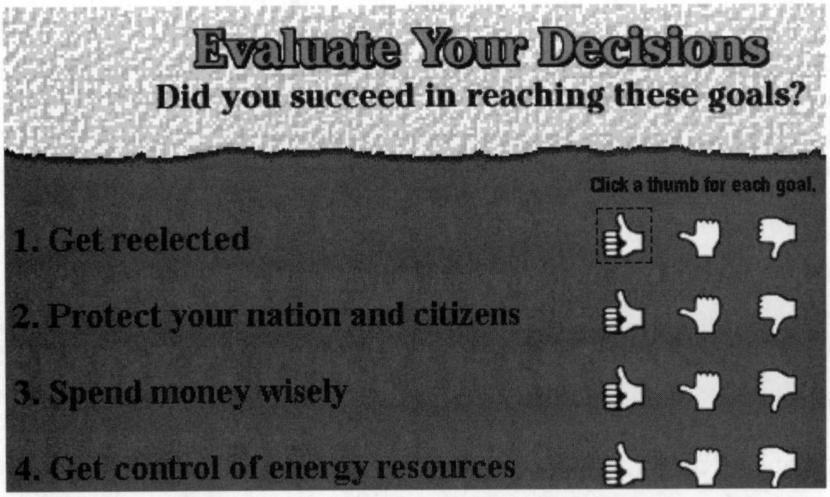

RECOMMENDED DISCUSSION-GENERATING SOFTWARE *(cont.)*

Decisions, Decisions by Tom Snyder Productions *(cont.)*

Titles Available

Ancient Empires

Grades 5–10

Students role-play the leader of a city-state and must struggle with the dilemmas of an ancient culture being overrun by an expanding empire. Topics covered include ancient civilization, famous battles, cultures, and roles of myths.

Feudalism

Grades 5–10

Students explore life during the Middle Ages by being put in the center of this dynamic world. In this turbulent world of shifting relationships, what was it like to be a feudal lord? Topics covered include the feudal system, crusades, medieval society, and the rise of towns and cities.

Building a Nation

Grades 5–10

The decline of European imperialism in the twentieth century welcomed scores of new nations in the world. Students role-play the leader of a newly independent country faced with many difficult issues. What kind of government will they establish? How will they stimulate the economy? Topics covered include nationalism, government, African history, economics, and colonialism.

Colonization

Grades 5–10

It's the future, and the world is facing an energy crisis. A private company has asked the president for funds to establish a colony in space, where it believes it will find new fuel deposits. Students learn the history of the colonization of America and apply it to this future dilemma. Topics covered include mercantilism, conflicting empires, and colonial life, commerce, and politics.

Immigration

Grades 5–10

Thousands of boat people from a war-torn area of the world are rapidly approaching the shores of the United States. Some of the refugees are fleeing political oppression; others are fleeing poverty. Students play the role of the president of the United States and learn to apply the lessons of the U.S. immigration policy. Topics covered include history of U.S. immigration, illegal immigration, economics, and politics.

Revolutionary Wars

Grades 5–10

Role-playing the governor of Catalan in the eastern province of Democ, students must decide whether or not to support a revolutionary movement among its citizens. Using information from the American Revolution and other revolutions around the world, students must decide how to bring the situation under control. Topics covered include the American Revolution, causes of revolutions, and revolutions in France, Russia, and China.

RECOMMENDED DISCUSSION-GENERATING SOFTWARE *(cont.)*

Decisions, Decisions by Tom Snyder Productions *(cont.)*

Titles Available *(cont.)*

The Cold War

Grades 5–10

As the leader of one of the world's two superpowers, students face a dilemma when a strategic ally requests help in quelling a popular internal rebellion. To make matters worse, the rival superpower supports the rebels. As the situation unfolds, students confront the same issues U.S. leaders met as they faced off with the Soviet Union after World War II. Topics covered include twentieth century history, world events, U.S. foreign policy, and international politics.

Campaign Trail

Grades 5–10

Students work through all the major issues faced by actual presidential candidates. Role-playing a bold third-party candidate, students rocket into the limelight and are immediately pressed for their positions on everything from the economy to health care to crime. Every move is critical! Topics covered include presidential elections, party politics, liberal vs. conservative policies, and the democratic process.

Town Government

Grades 5–10

When the residents of a small American town face a large and unforeseen dilemma, how do they resolve the problem? Role-playing the mayor of Alpine, students weigh the pros and cons of Malaco, a local mining company, and its expansion. In the process, students discover how much authority rests in the hands of the mayor, government committees, and residents. Topics covered include local government, civic responsibility, town meetings, citizenship, and democracy.

The Environment

Grades 5–10

The headlines of Alpine's local paper cry outrage about the town's polluted pond. Role-playing the mayor of Alpine, students must tackle the situation. Students interpret science and apply what they learn to make public policy decisions. They experience political trade-offs that accompany any course of action. Topics covered include pollution, land use, economics and the environment, and local and global environments.

Lying, Cheating, Stealing

Grades 5–10

Eighty percent of high school students say that cheating on exams is always wrong; yet, sixty percent of these same high school students admit they have cheated within the past year. Most kids know that lying, cheating, and stealing are wrong; however, many still do these things. We want students to constantly ask, "What is the right thing to do?" And we want to instill in them the integrity to act according to the answer. Topics covered include responsibility, caring for others, honesty, respect, and morality.

RECOMMENDED DISCUSSION-GENERATING SOFTWARE *(cont.)*

Decisions, Decisions by Tom Snyder Productions *(cont.)*

Titles Available *(cont.)*

Substance Abuse

Grades 4–10

"Just say No!" Is it really that easy? In this activity, students confront peer pressure, responsible versus irresponsible behavior, and relationships with authority. Students learn to set goals, look at facts, weigh divergent points of view, and, in the end, make decisions and face consequences. Topics covered include substance abuse, peer pressure, and responsible behavior.

Prejudice

Grades 5–10

Students learn and talk about prejudice, discrimination, and the processes that perpetuate these ideas in a non-threatening environment. Students role-play the mayor of Spring Falls whose re-election looks guaranteed until the controversy over Ray's Antiques & Stuff. Ray sells items that many people think perpetuate racist attitudes. Townspeople disagree on what the mayor should do, while political opponents have started to make this a central issue in the campaign. Topics covered include the First Amendment, racism, civil rights, government, and civics.

Violence in the Media

Grades 5–10

Our society is full of violence, and so is our media. Is there a relationship? Does the violence that bombards the airwaves fuel the violence that feeds the headlines? In *Violence in the Media*, students take the role of an advertising executive for a company that is sponsoring "City Street," a controversial television special about life in a gang-infested urban neighborhood. Previews of the program spark mixed reviews. Is the show too violent? Or is it simply realistic? As an advertising executive, what is the responsible thing to do? Topics covered include television violence, free speech, censorship, and the television industry.

The Constitution

Grades 5–10

This title brings students face to face with the dilemmas, compromises, and struggles of writing the American Constitution. Students live in a fictional confederation that is plagued with many of the same problems America faced in the 1780's—huge debts, border threats, a currency crisis, trade disputes, and internal rebellion, and a weak national government. They must draft a constitution that will alleviate these problems for now and the future.

BUILDING SKILLS

One of the more popular uses of the classroom computer is for skill building or concept reinforcement. Many of these programs are engaging, motivating, and challenging, all while reinforcing specific skills. There is drill and practice software available in almost all subject areas, such as phonics, vocabulary building, multiplication facts, states and capitals, and more. As educators, we know that drill and practice lessons are valuable to all students. Why not let the computer do some of this work for you? Later in this chapter, there are hundreds of software suggestions for a variety of subject areas.

CHOOSING THE RIGHT SOFTWARE

There is so much software available, and sometimes it can be overwhelming to you as an educator. To truly integrate technology into the classroom curriculum, the teacher has to choose the software while keeping in mind how it could be integrated into the curriculum. Here are some tips for choosing the right software for your classroom.

- Decide which skills you want the software to reinforce. Choose software based on the skills. Some software comes with a scope and sequence.
- Check out the grade level and ability level of the software.
- Ask colleagues about software which has been successful in their classrooms. Try the software on their computers to see if you like it before you buy it.
- Order a demo version of the software to test it in your classroom before making a major purchase. Most companies will send you a free demo copy if you ask.
- Many teachers' magazines have software reviews. Try to read a review about the software, preferably not from the company who is selling it, before purchasing it.
- When ordering software, make sure you know if your computer is a Mac or a PC.
- If you do not have a CD-ROM, make sure you can order the software on floppy disk. If you do have a CD-ROM, it is better to order the software in the CD-ROM version.
- Check to see if the software comes with a rebate. Many software companies offer rebates of ten or twenty dollars. Ask the vendor or the sales clerk.
- Investigate the technical support for the software in case you run into a problem.

BUILDING SKILLS *(cont.)*

EDUCATIONAL SOFTWARE PACKAGING

There are several ways in which educational software is packaged for school use. Read the following choices carefully to make sure that you are spending computer dollars wisely.

Home Version-Consumer Version

It includes one disk and no teaching materials.

School Version

It includes one disk and a teacher manual which usually includes online and offline classroom material for the use with the program. Most have lesson plans, templates, and blackline masters.

Lab Pack

It usually includes five disks and teacher materials. Some lab packs are available with ten or more disks. The price makes this a good school purchase for 5 or 10 computers. Teams of teachers may want combine their efforts and resources to purchase a lab pack which may be shared. Often a lab pack is only twice the cost of the school version even though it includes five copies of the program instead of one.

Site License

Permission is granted for legally copying the program for every computer in a specific building or district. It includes teacher materials and is a good choice for schools with many computers. Some site licenses are for an unlimited number of copies; however, others are for a specific number.

Network Version

This indicates the program has been specifically formatted so that it can be installed on the network and shared with all of the networked computers. Check with the computer person at your school to see if this would be a good option for your school.

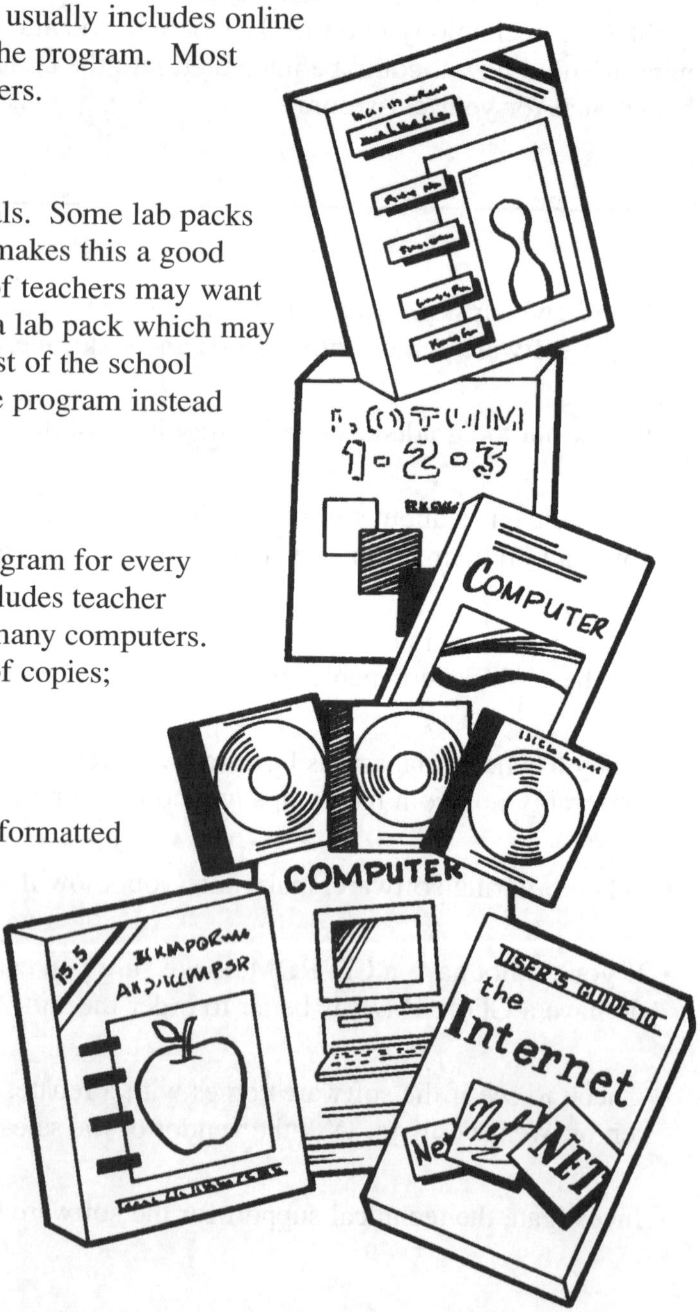

SOFTWARE EVALUATION RATING SHEET

Program Name: ______________________________

Grade Level: ______________________________

Subject Area: ______________________________

	Poor		Deficient		Sufficient		Desirable		Exemplary	
Content: Alignment with curriculum	1	2	3	4	5	6	7	8	9	10
Appropriate for grade level	1	2	3	4	5	6	7	8	9	10
Accuracy	1	2	3	4	5	6	7	8	9	10
Ease of Use: Easy program loading	1	2	3	4	5	6	7	8	9	10
Simple screen directions	1	2	3	4	5	6	7	8	9	10
Program Appearance: Uncluttered screen	1	2	3	4	5	6	7	8	9	10
Material clearly presented	1	2	3	4	5	6	7	8	9	10
Learning Style: Uses more than one modality	1	2	3	4	5	6	7	8	9	10
Support: Technical support #	1	2	3	4	5	6	7	8	9	10
Teacher manual with activities	1	2	3	4	5	6	7	8	9	10

Hardware: ____________

Printer compatibility: ____________

Memory needed: ____________

Needs hard disk? ____________

Computer compatibility: ____________

Peripherals needed: ____________

SKILL-BUILDING SOFTWARE EXAMPLES

There is so much skill-building software available that it would impossible to highlight all it. However, it is important to understand the value of this type of software, especially in the one-computer classroom. On the next several pages, a few of the more popular skill-building pieces of software are highlighted.

Reading Blaster by Knowledge Adventure

There are three levels of *Reading Blaster: Ages 4–6, 6–9,* and *9–12*. Students will encounter a universe of sounds, words, sentences, and stories in *Reading Blaster: Ages 4–6*. Each surprise-filled planet features engaging phonics and word-building activities designed to help students learn to read and to develop writing and spelling skills. In the *Reading Blaster: Ages 6–9,* students learn over 2,000 new vocabulary words, silent letters, compound and rhyming words, and parts of speech. The advanced *Reading Blaster* strengthens reading comprehension skills as students learn to read for details, find the main idea, make inferences, draw conclusions, and build vocabulary. A step-by-step approach and adjustable skill levels ensure that your students will be reading like champions.

SKILL-BUILDING SOFTWARE EXAMPLES *(cont.)*

Kid Phonics by Knowledge Adventure

There are two levels of *Kid Phonics*. In *Kid Phonics 1,* students progress from hearing the sounds that make up words to actually reading the words themselves. *Kid Phonics 1* promotes correct spelling while building vocabulary. Students will confidently progress into *Kid Phonics 2* as they move from sounding out words to building whole sentences. Students learn to understand prefixes, suffixes, silent letters, and more.

SKILL-BUILDING SOFTWARE EXAMPLES *(cont.)*

Graph Club Machine by Tom Snyder Productions

Graphs are a powerful addition to the written word. The *Graph Club* is an easy-to-use graphing tool which can be used for self-directed exploration, presentations, or creative class projects. Students using *Graph Club* learn to gather, sort, and classify information. Then they construct graphs, analyze their data, and print their graphs in multiple sizes. The *Graph Club* assists children in making the transition from graphing with manipulatives to graphing in the abstract and helps them understand the relationships among different representations of the graph and table. Students learn to use graphs to solve problems and make decisions.

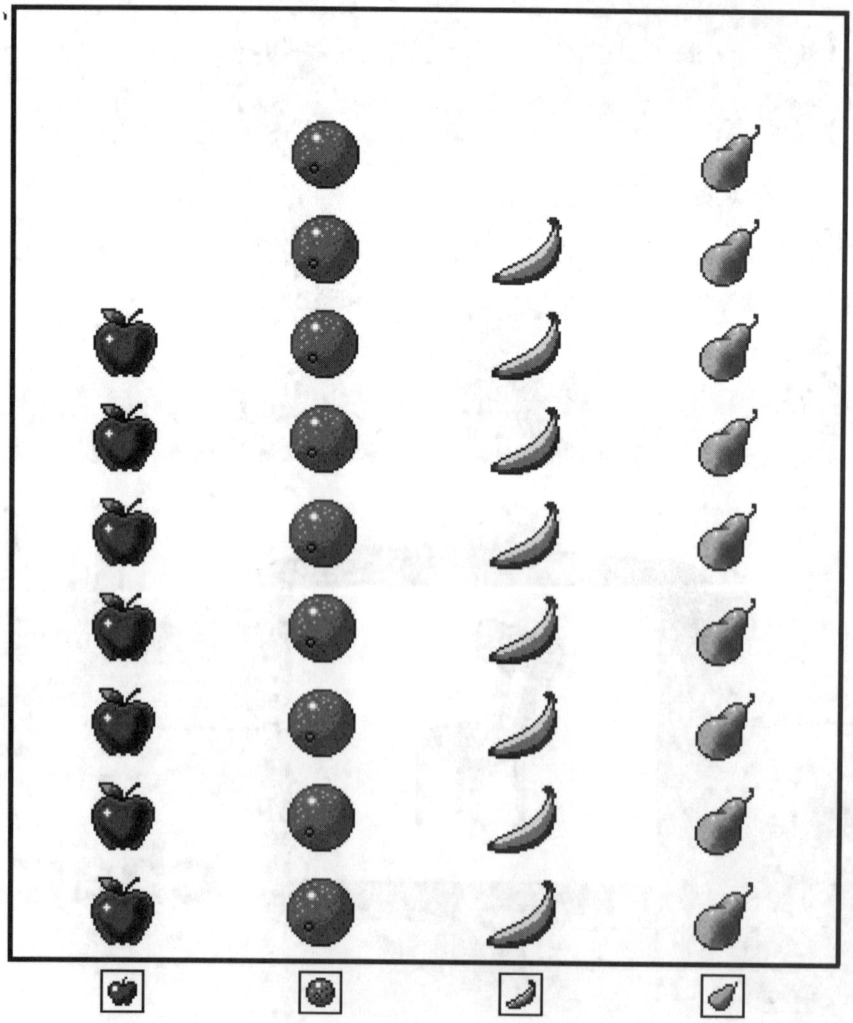

SKILL-BUILDING SOFTWARE EXAMPLES *(cont.)*

Math Blaster by Knowledge Adventure

There are six levels of *Math Blaster,* ranging from age four all the way through pre-algebra and geometry. In *Math Blaster 4–6,* step-by-step methods build essential math and thinking skills in students. As the *Math Blaster* series progresses, students master computation skills, estimation, and number patterns and build problem-solving skills. The *Math Blaster* series for older students reinforces computation with decimals, integers, and rational numbers. Students begin to understand ratios, proportions, and percents. *Math Blaster Geometry* covers all of the basics of geometry, including shapes, proofs, area, volume, formulas, and logic. Customizing the program allows the teacher to target specific subject areas and levels of difficulty. Progress reports help students set and keep their goals.

SKILL-BUILDING SOFTWARE EXAMPLES *(cont.)*

Jump Start Adventure by Knowledge Adventure

The *Jump Start Learning System* is designed to cover all the major subjects taught in each particular grade from preschool through fifth grade. In the early grades of *Jump Start,* students practice phonic skills, read and comprehend stories, solve math problems, and discover more about science, art, and music. In the *Jump Start Second Grade* and *Jump Start Third Grade,* students practice writing and composition, build grammar skills, develop higher math skills, and explore U.S. geography. In the fourth and fifth grades, students discriminate amoung parts of speech, develop logical thinking skills, solve complex math equations, and learn fractions and decimals.

SKILL-BUILDING SOFTWARE EXAMPLES *(cont.)*

Neighborhood Map Machine by Tom Snyder Productions

This easy-to-use map-making tool enables students to create, navigate, and print maps of their own neighborhood, other communities, or imaginary places, using objects such as roads, trees, buildings, and parks. As students map out their towns, they learn essential geography skills, including compass direction, distance and scale, grid coordinates, and symbols. Students can customize their own maps by adding photographs and movies of buildings in their town.

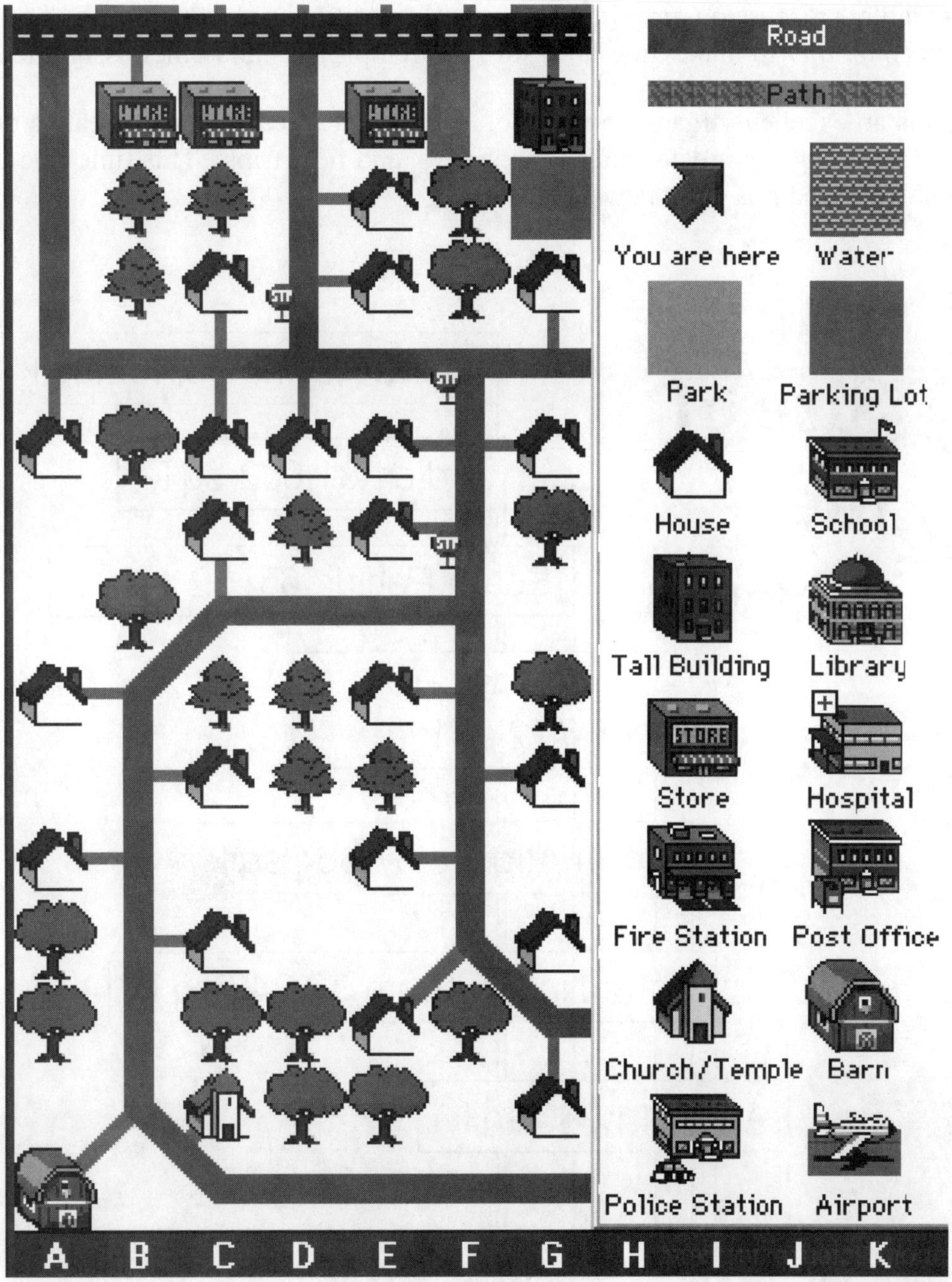

SKILL-BUILDING SOFTWARE EXAMPLES *(cont.)*

TimeLiner by Tom Snyder Productions

Time lines have long been considered a valuable tool for teaching many subject areas. *TimeLiner* is a practical, easy-to-use tool for creating and printing time lines of historical, contemporary, and future events. With *TimeLiner,* students can construct banner time lines that wrap around the classroom or extend along a hall in your school. Or, you can print single-page time lines for handy reference and display on a bulletin board.

The teacher can easily involve the whole class in creating a time line in order to introduce students to new material, stimulate discussion, or reinforce facts. In addition, pairs or small groups of students may want to use *TimeLiner* to make time lines for research projects and other assignments.

Also, *TimeLiner* is an excellent organizational tool for teachers. Teachers can create a time line of the quarter or semester, listing exam dates, papers, holidays, and field trips. This time line could be posted in the classroom or printed in a class newsletter.

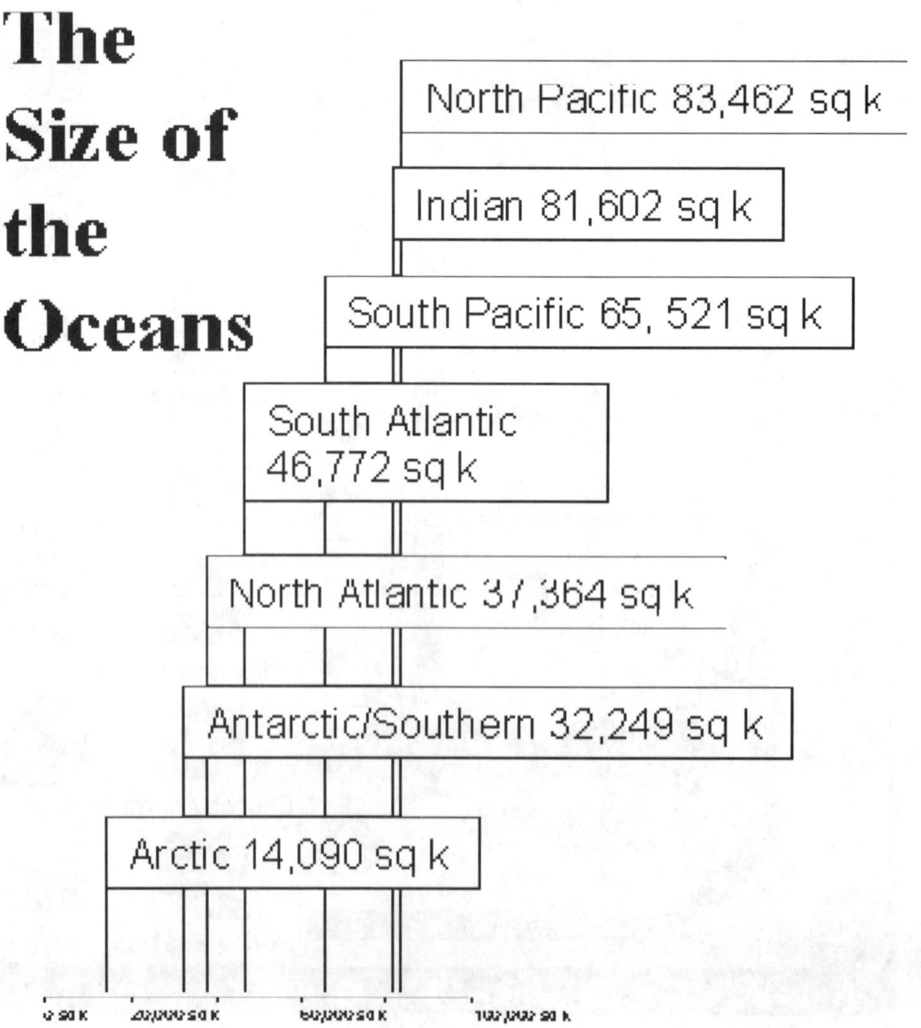

ART AND MUSIC SKILL-BUILDING SOFTWARE

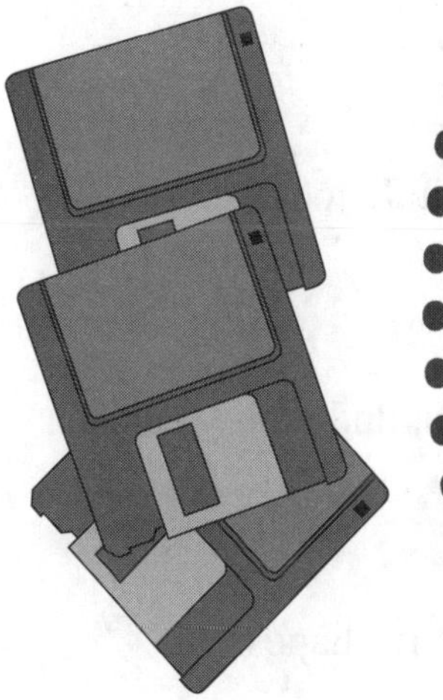

MUSIC

Title: *Miracle Piano*
Publisher: Mindscape
This sequential set of music teaching programs teach the skills of piano playing.

Title: *Piano Discovery for Kids*
Publisher: Jump Music
With this program, students learn to play the piano. Contents include keyboard basics, finger exercises, performance skills, rhythm, and note reading.

Title: *Play It by Ear*
Publisher: Alfred Publishing
Beginning through advanced students practice ear training with the aid of an on-screen piano keyboard and guitar fret board.

Title: *Practical Musica*
Publisher: ARS Nova Software
Students receive training for music theory.

Title: *The Treehouse*
Publisher: Brøderbund Software
Students explore and make discoveries about music, science, mathematics, and language.

VISUAL ARTS

Title: *Art Lesson* by Tomie dePaola
Publisher: Learning Company
With a click of the mouse, students can enjoy Tomie dePaola's beloved story filled with lively animations and sounds, exciting art activities, and a video interview with the author.

Title: *Magic Artist*
Publisher: Disney
In this ultimate art studio, students learn to create and draw just like a Disney artist. The program includes six interactive drawing lessons.

EARLY CHILDHOOD/PRESCHOOL SKILL-BUILDING SOFTWARE

Title: *A to Zap!*
Publisher: Sunburst Communications
Children learn about letters, numbers, and words as they explore the 26 letters of the alphabet.

Title: *Clock Works*
Publisher: Learning Company
Practice telling time using both analog and digital clocks.

Title: *Hop to It!*
Publisher: Sunburst Communications
Practice number lines with addition, subtraction, and equivalencies.

Title: *JumpStart PreSchool*
Publisher: Knowledge Adventure
Introduce children to colors, letters, numbers, and shapes.

Title: *Kids Time Deluxe*
Publisher: Great Wave Software
Five games and puzzles develop early reading, computer, and music skills.

Title: *Muppet Math*
Publisher: Sunburst Communications
Muppets introduce primary math problems in a variety of real-world settings.

Title: *My Silly CD of ABC's, Colors, Counting, and Opposites.*
Publisher: Harmony Interactive
Four different CD-ROMs teach ABC's, colors, counting, and opposites. Sound effects and bright illustrations enhance learning.

Title: *Reader Rabbit*
Publisher: Learning Company
Beginning reading skills are taught and reinforced using the C-V-C approach.

Title: *Sesame Street: Get Set to Learn*
Publisher: Creative Wonders
Young children develop thinking and problem-solving skills as well as a variety of kindergarten readiness skills with the assistance of the Sesame Street muppets.

KEYBOARDING SKILL-BUILDING SOFTWARE

Title: *JumpStart Typing*
Publisher: Knowledge Adventure
Students learn typing skills while competing in the ultimate high-tech pentathlon. Students learn correct typing skills, hand placement, and posture (thirty lessons).

Title: *Kid Keys*
Publisher: Knowledge Adventure
Three activities provide a playful, interactive environment that helps students progress from learning key positions to typing smoothly and accurately (encourages early reading skills).

Title: *Mario Teaches Typing*
Publisher: Interplay Productions
A variety of game-like activities are designed to maintain and reinforce keyboarding skills.

Title: *Mavis Beacon Teaches Typing*
Publisher: Mindscape
This keyboarding program focuses on word and letter combinations.

Title: *Slam Dunk Typing*
Publisher: Creative Wonders
Dribble, jump, dunk and type! All the action of arcade basketball combined with a 10-level keyboarding tutor to build accuracy, rhythm, and speed.

Title: *Stickybear Typing*
Publisher: Optimum Resources
Three exercises give instruction and practice in keyboarding skills.

Title: *Type*
Publisher: Brøderbund
This features performance graphs, customized exercises, and games for students practicing keyboarding with real words, not random letters.

Title: *Type to Learn*
Publisher: Sunburst Communications
This language-based approach to keyboarding provides practice in spelling and composition.

LANGUAGE ARTS SKILL-BUILDING SOFTWARE

Title: *Bailey's Bookhouse*
Publisher: Edmark
Students learn letters, acquire vocabulary, make rhymes, and publish their own books starring Bailey and his neighborhood friends.

Title: *English Express Deluxe*
Publisher: Knowledge Adventure
With this comprehensive multimedia approach to ESL, students listen, speak, read, and write English in a relevant context.

Title: *Grammar Games*
Publisher: Knowledge Adventure
With four engaging activities, students of all ages master key grammar skills as they save the rain forest from destruction and uncover its hidden wonders.

Title: *Kid Phonics 1* and *Kid Phonics 2*
Publisher: Knowledge Adventure
Activities develop auditory awareness of letter sounds, establish connections between sounds and letter clusters, and teach prefixes, suffixes, and silent letters.

Title: *Memory Building Blocks*
Publisher: Sunburst Communications
Practice memory strategies in six concentration games: pictures, graphics, words, colors, shapes, patterns, and tunes.

Title: *Muppets on Stage*
Publisher: Sunburst Communications
Students learn the alphabet and numbers with Kermit and the whole gang. Toggle between Spanish and English.

Title: *Reader Rabbit*
Publisher: Learning Company
Beginning reading skills are taught and reinforced using the C-V-C approach.

Title: *Reader Rabbit's Reading Development Library*
Publisher: Learning Company
A journey through twenty imaginative Letter Lands takes students to skill houses that will help them read storybooks.

LANGUAGE ARTS SKILL-BUILDING SOFTWARE *(cont.)*

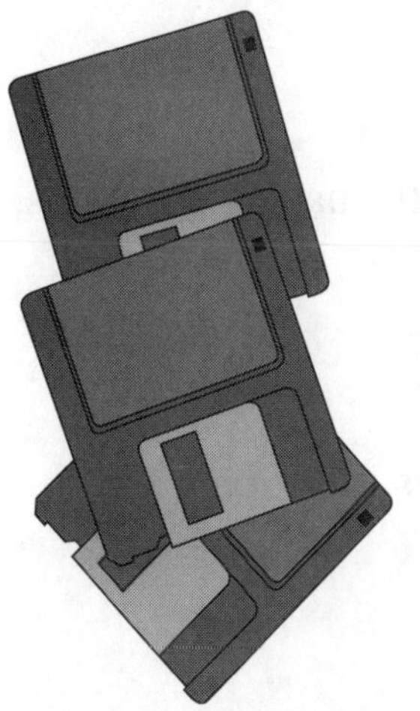

Title: *Reading Blaster Ages 4–6, 6–9,* and *9–12*
Publisher: Knowledge Adventure
Students learn sight words, phonic sounds, and letter blends. In Ages 6-9, basic reading skills are mastered. Ages 9–12 strengthens vocabulary and reading comprehension.

Title: *Reading Who? Reading You!*
Publisher: Sunburst Communications
Students decode words and engage in activities and puzzles as they develop phonetic reading skills.

Title: *Stickybear Reading Comprehension*
Publisher: Optimum Resources
Familiar Stickybear reinforces reading comprehension as it explores stories pertaining to science, such as the invention of Velcro, the digestive system, and fossils.

Title: *Super Solvers' Spellbound*
Publisher: Learning Company
These spelling games have adventure themes.

Title: *Tronic Phonics*
Publisher: Macmillan/McGraw-Hill
This program encourages students to read a story, listen to the words containing phonograms, discover new rhyming words, read aloud, and record a rhyme.

Title: *Ultimate Speed Reader*
Publisher: Knowledge Adventure
Six challenging activities help students increase reading speed and comprehension.

Title: *Ultimate Word Attack*
Publisher: Knowledge Adventure
Through five activities, students learn definitions and spellings of over 3,200 words.

Title: *Word Munchers Deluxe*
Publisher: Learning Company
Students develop word-attack strategies and word-recognition skills as they race a Muncher around a 3-D grid to gobble objects and words.

Title: *Words Around Me*
Publisher: Edmark
Designed to help student identify 275 words, this program has plurals of people, places, things, and actions in both Spanish and English.

MATH SKILL-BUILDING SOFTWARE

Algebra

Title: *Math Blaster: Algebra*
Publisher: Knowledge Adventure
Students must successfully solve algebraic expressions and equations, plot points on a graph, and factor polynomials to fight the strange alien forces.

Title: *Math Blaster: Pre-Algebra*
Publisher: Knowledge Adventure
Students solve tricky word problems, create mathematical equations, and compute fractions, decimals, and integers.

Title: *Math Connections I*
Publisher: Sunburst Communications
Students work with objects that display variables, functions, and graphs.

Title: *Math Connections II*
Publisher: Sunburst Communications
Student manipulate objects to visualize mathematical relationships as they are introduced to higher-level algebra concepts.

Geometry/Measurement

Title: *3D Transformation*
Publisher: Intellimation
Students practice scaling, translating, and rotating objects to match a target object.

Title: *Math Blaster: Geometry*
Publisher: Knowledge Adventure
Understanding of triangles, angles, and the Pythagorean theorem is reinforced. Students learn the properties of polygons, practice proofs, and explore area and volume.

Title: *Mighty Math*
Publisher: Edmark
Students explore basic geometry principles in an animated world of math adventure.

MATH SKILL-BUILDING SOFTWARE *(cont.)*

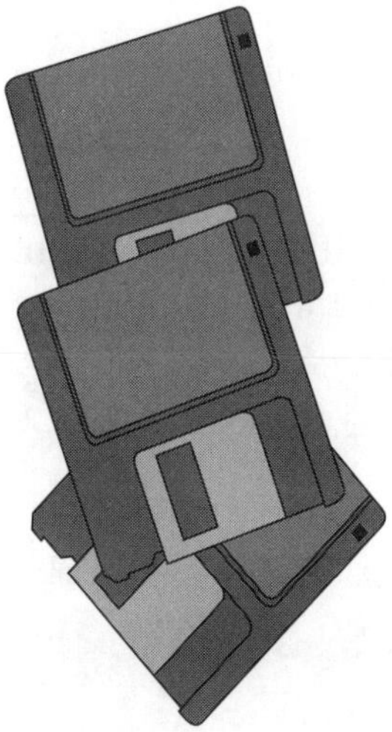

Number Concepts

Title: *Balancing Bear*
Publisher: Sunburst Communications
Students manipulate numbers as weights to balance Bear's beam, developing a sense of understanding of equivalence.

Title: *Coin Critters*
Publisher: Nordic
Students develop an understanding of money by learning the face values of coins and purchasing, matching, and counting back change on several different levels of difficulty.

Title: *Fraction Attraction*
Publisher: Sunburst Communications
A series of activities involves different uses of fractions.

Title: *Fraction Munchers*
Publisher: Learning Company
Students learn fractional numbers, equivalent fractions, and expressions in a game format.

Title: *Lost Mind of Dr. Brain*
Publisher: Knowledge Adventure
This mind-bending game is based on Howard Gardner's theory of multiple intelligences. Students are challenged to solve hundreds of complex interactive puzzles involving language, logic, music, art, physics, chemistry, and more.

Title: *Math Blaster Ages 4–6*
Publisher: Knowledge Adventure
Students master essential early math skills, learn numbers and quantities, practice addition and subtraction, and learn greater than and less than.

Title: *Math Blaster Ages 6–9*
Publisher: Knowledge Adventure
Students practice addition, subtraction, multiplication, and division while building problem-solving skills. Students gain an understanding of fractions, decimals, and percents.

Title: *Math Blaster Ages 9–12*
Publisher: Knowledge Adventure
Students practice larger number addition, subtraction, multiplication, and division while building a foundation for pre-algebra. Fractions, decimals, and percents are all reinforced.

MATH SKILL-BUILDING SOFTWARE *(cont.)*

Number Concepts *(cont.)*

Title: *Math for the Real World*
Publisher: Knowledge Adventure
Students build word-problem-solving skills with everyday math situations. An awareness of math usage in the real world is fostered.

Title: *Math Workshop*
Publisher: Broderbund
Students practice fractions, pattern recognition, addition, subtraction, multiplication, division, and problem-solving skills through creative games.

Title: *Muppet Math*
Publisher: Sunburst Communications
Muppets introduce primary math problems in a variety of real-world settings.

Title: *Number Munchers*
Publisher: Learning Company
Students guide the Muncher through grids, looking for numbers that meet a given arithmetic criterion.

Title: *Puzzle Tanks*
Publisher: Sunburst Communications
Students practice math and logic skills by filling a large tank from a number of smaller tanks.

Title: *Time Warp of Dr. Brain*
Publisher: Knowledge Adventure
Students get an amazing mental workout as they travel through the past, present, and future to solve 600 interactive puzzles.

Title: *Treasure Galaxy*
Publisher: Learning Company
Activities develop math and critical-thinking skills.

Title: *Troggle Trouble Math*
Publisher: Learning Company
Students solve word problems at various locations in the adventure and stump the Troggles.

SCIENCE SKILL-BUILDING SOFTWARE

Title: *3-D Atlas*
Publisher: Creative Wonders
Explore our planet, navigate around the globe, and study changes in the Earth's composition over time, using this comprehensive atlas.

Title: *3-D Dinosaur Adventure*
Publisher: Knowledge Adventure
Using 3-D glasses, students experience high-resolution motion pictures as they journey back in time to study fossils and dinosaurs.

Title: *Amazing Animals*
Publisher: DK Multimedia
Students are introduced to the animal kingdom with a guided tour, games, creative activities, and online connections.

Title: *Amazon Trail*
Publisher: Learning Company
In a simulation of a trip up the Amazon in search of a cure for malaria, students meet historical figures and explore the rain forest environment.

Title: *Animals and How They Grow*
Publisher: National Geographic
Students learn life cycles of animals from mammals to insects

Title: *Body Works*
Publisher: Learning Company
This multimedia tour of the human body includes 3-D images, definitions of over 1,200 medical terms, pronunciations of over 1,900 technical terms, and live-action video on vital medical subjects.

Title: *Eyewitness Encyclopedia of Nature*
Publisher: DK Multimedia
This is a multimedia reference guide to the natural world.

SCIENCE SKILL-BUILDING SOFTWARE *(cont.)*

Title: *Eyewitness Encyclopedia of Science*
Publisher: DK Multimedia
This multimedia reference guide to science and technology covers math, physics, chemistry, and life science. It also contains experts in these fields and a quiz master.

Title: *Eyewitness Encyclopedia of Space and the Universe*
Publisher: DK Multimedia
This eference guide to astronomy, space exploration, and the cosmos provides information on the planets, stars, galaxies, astronauts, spacecraft, satellites, and probes.

Title: *GeoSafari Science*
Publisher: Educational Insight
Embark on unique learning adventures answering hundreds of questions on physical and natural sciences!

Title: *Gizmos and Gadgets*
Publisher: Learning Company
Science activities based on principles of observation and experimentation include force, magnets, electricity, gears, balance, energy, and machines.

Title: *How Your Body Works*
Publisher: Mindscape
Students learn about their bodies from the inside out; featured is a straight-talk approach to anatomy and physiology with a major focus on the 12 body systems.

Title: *Insects*
Publisher: Arch Publisher's Group
In this interactive nature experience students learn about insects and their habitats.

Title: *The Magic School Bus Explores the Human Body*
Publisher: Microsoft
Join Ms. Frizzle and the class on a wacky trip through the human body; explore how the human body works and discover the way out.

Title: *The Magic School Bus Explores the Ocean*
Publisher: Microsoft
Explore seven ocean zones and solve the clues to find the sunken treasure. Conduct experiments that make science fun and easy to understand.

SCIENCE SKILL-BUILDING SOFTWARE *(cont.)*

Title: *Operation Neptune*
Publisher: The Learning Company
Students take the helm of a hi-tech submarine on a mission to save the Earth from a mysterious toxin. Students make their way by interpreting charts, maps, and graphs.

Title: *Science Blaster Junior*
Publisher: Knowledge Adventure
Provided in this program is an overall introduction to science, covering topics such as weather, animal classification, sequencing, and magnetism.

Title: *Science in Your Ear*
Publisher: Learning Company
Scientific properties of sound can be explored using sound waves, musical instruments, and how the human ear hears sound.

Title: *Super Munchers*
Publisher: Learning Company
This is an enjoyable activity for learning about categories such as food, nutrition, world geography, and famous people.

Title: *The Way Things Work*
Publisher: DK Multimedia
Based on the David Macauley book, this program contains animations and audio explanations of the workings of many technologies. Included is a selection of inventors and scientists and connections to the Internet.

Title: *Thinkin' Science Zap!*
Publisher: Edmark
Interactive learning labs let students explore principles of light, sound, and electricity. The program includes a multimedia science encyclopedia, articles, illustrations, and simple experiments.

Title: *Ultimate Human Body*
Publisher: DK Multimedia
Students explore the systems of the human body through 3-D, 2-D, and x-ray views of the body with complete audio directions.

Title: *Ultimate 3-D Skeleton*
Publisher: DK Multimedia
With this basic guide to human skeleton, students learn about bones, examine them in 3-D, and take a quiz to test their knowledge.

SOCIAL STUDIES SKILL-BUILDING SOFTWARE

Title: *Amazon Trail*
Publisher: Learning Company
In a simulation of a trip up the Amazon in search of a cure for malaria, students meet historical figures and explore the rain forest environment.

Title: *Capitol Hill*
Publisher: Mindscape
Students explore life on Capitol Hill; included is an insider's tour of the capitol.

Title: *Cartopedia: The Ultimate World Reference Atlas*
Publisher: DK Multimedia
Students access a world atlas of 193 countries through maps, pictures, tables and charts of comparison data, and interactive articles.

Title: *Castle Explorer*
Publisher: DK Multimedia
Through an adventure, students gain an insight into how people lived in a fourteenth century castle.

Title: *Children's Atlas of the United States*
Publisher: Rand McNally
Maps with animated markers show state capitals, largest cities, rivers and mountain, graphs, charts, animations, and text for each state.

Title: *Explore Yellowstone*
Publisher: Learning Company
Students take a multimedia journey through Yellowstone National Park, exploring ecology, geology, geography, and its history along the way.

itle: *Eyewitness History of the World*
Publisher: DK Multimedia
This is an extensive multimedia reference guide about the history of the world.

Title: *GeoSafari: Geography*
Publisher: Educational Insights
This multimedia quiz game takes students on a whirlwind tour of the world. Hundreds of questions and answers teach continents, countries, states, landmarks, currencies, flags, and world greetings.

SOCIAL STUDIES SKILL-BUILDING SOFTWARE (cont.)

Title: *His Name Was Lincoln*
Publisher: Sunburst Communications
Students visit American history from 1809 to 1865 as it relates to President Lincoln. Included are copies of original documents, excellent narration, and rich photographs.

Title: *How Would You Survive?*
Publisher: Grolier Education
Students travel through time and experience life as it was for the Ancient Egyptians, Aztecs, and Vikings.

Title: *Imagination Express Destination: Pyramids*
Publisher: Edmark
Students create their own interactive books and movies featuring pharaohs, mummies, and life on the Nile, while building writing, creativity, and communication skills.

Title: *Imagination Express Destination: Time Trip, USA*
Publisher: Edmark
Students create imaginative stories about a fictional New England town, using images and characters from various time zones beginning in the 1600s.

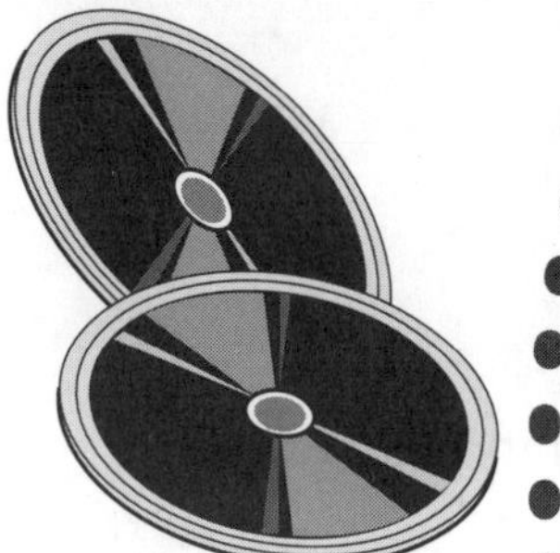

Title: *MayaQuest*
Publisher: Learning Company
Students develop decision-making, problem-solving, and cooperative-learning skills as they travel with an anthropological expedition through Yucatan and ancient Mayan civilizations.

Title: *My First Amazing World Explorer*
Publisher: DK Multimedia
This is a young child's introduction to maps, atlases, and the world.

Title: *Oregon Trail*
Publisher: Learning Company
Students venture through a simulation of the 1850 trek west in a covered wagon. Students can also travel the Oregon Trail with other students via the Internet.

Title: *Trudy's Time and Place House*
Publisher: Edmark
Five activities teach time, geography, map skills, and direction.

SOCIAL STUDIES SKILL-BUILDING SOFTWARE *(cont.)*

Title: *Vietnam War*
Publisher: Intellimation
This program contains interviews with war veterans, sound effects, animation, quotations, maps, charts, and movie reviews about the Vietnam War.

Title: *Vital Links*
Publisher: Knowledge Adventure
This comprehensive U.S. history curriculum deals with immigration, industrialization, the Spanish-American War, World War I, and voting rights.

Title: *Where in the USA is Carmen Sandiego?*
Publisher: Brøderbund Software
Students follow clues and use Fodor's USA Travel Guide to capture Carmen Sandiego.

Title: *Where in the World is Carmen Sandiego?*
Publisher: Brøderbund Software
Use the World Almanac to search the world and capture Carmen.

Title: *Where in the World is Carmen Sandiego, Jr.*
Publisher: Brøderbund Software
This is a simplified version of the geography game for younger students.

Title: *Where in Time is Carmen Sandiego?*
Publisher: Brøderbund Software
Cover 1,500 years of history as students travel through time to capture Carmen.

Title: *Yukon Trail*
Publisher: Learning Company
Students develop reading comprehension and problem-solving skills as they join the historical simulation set during the Alaskan Gold Rush of 1897.

WORLD LANGUAGES SKILL-BUILDING SOFTWARE

Title: *Berlitz Language Series—French, German, Spanish*
Publisher: Berlitz
French, German, and Spanish are made easy using the real-life situations in this program. Students will learn to speak, write and understand up to 12,500 foreign words. Tests allow students to chart their progress as they advance from novices to fluent speakers.

Title: *ClarisWorks Spanish*
Publisher: Apple Education
This is the complete integrated *ClarisWorks* package in Spanish.

Title: *English Express Deluxe*
Publisher: Knowledge Adventure
With this comprehensive multimedia approach to ESL students listen, speak, read, and write English in a relevant context.

Title: *French to Go*
Publisher: Creative Multimedia
This program contains over 60 minutes of instruction video and a talking dictionary. Students learn French using conversational phrases, games, and exercises.

Title: *Japanese to Go*
Publisher: Creative Multimedia
With over 60 minutes of instruction video and a talking dictionary, students learn Japanese using conversational phrases, games, and exercises.

Title: *JumpStart Spanish*
Publisher: Knowledge Adventure
Inside a colorful clubhouse, young students are exposed to Spanish vocabulary, culture, and music. Over 200 words and dozens of phrases and songs are introduced.

Title: *Learn to Speak English*
Publisher: Learning Company
This program contains 30 English lessons with four native speakers and includes drills on English.

Title: *Learn to Speak French*
Publisher: Learning Company
This program contains 36 French lessons with five native French it speakers and allows you to record your own voice and compare to speaker's voice.

WORLD LANGUAGES SKILL-BUILDING SOFTWARE *(cont.)*

Title: *Learn to Speak Spanish*
Publisher: Learning Company
This program contains 30 Spanish lessons with five native speakers in real-world situations and includes drills on Spanish grammar.

Title: *Practice Makes Perfect: French*
Publisher: Learning Company
These beginner and intermediate activities in French include over 2,300 everyday words in context, practice videos, audio with native speakers, and vocabulary and pronunciation work.

Title: *Practice Makes Perfect: German*
Publisher: Learning Company
These beginner and intermediate activities in German include over 2,300 everyday words in context, practice videos, audio with native speakers, and vocabulary and pronunciation work.

Title: *Practice Makes Perfect: Spanish*
Publisher: Learning Company
These beginner and intermediate activities in Spanish include over 2,300 everyday words in context, practice videos, audio with native speakers, and vocabulary and pronunciation work.

Title: *Pronunciation Tutor-Chinese*
Publisher: Learning Company
Students are introduced to basic pronunciation guidelines and hear the pronunciation of native speakers. It is also available in French, German, and Spanish.

Title: *Rosetta Stone: French*
Publisher: Fairfield Language Technologies
Students learn French through phrases based on real-world photographs, patterning, and discrimination skills. It is also available in German, Russian, and Spanish.

Title: *Spanish to Go*
Publisher: Creative Multimedia
This program contains over 60 minutes of instruction video and a talking dictionary. Students learn Spanish using conversational phrases, games, and exercises.

Title: *Storybook Weaver: Spanish Version*
Publisher: Learning Company
This program emphasizes process writing to help students write stories in Spanish.

EDUCATIONAL SOFTWARE PUBLISHERS

The following companies specialize in software for the school setting for grades Pre–K through 12. You should find their sales personnel extremely knowledgeable in helping you make your software choices. Most companies distribute catalogs and would be pleased to add you to their mailing lists.

Alfred Publishing
(800) 625-3733

Apple Education
(800) 747-7483

Arch Publisher's Group (Educorp)
(800) 843-9497

ARS Nova Software
(800) 445-4866

Berlitz Language Co.
(800) 526-8047

Brøderbund
(800) 521-6263

Creative Wonders (order from Learning Co.)
(800) 852-2255

DK Multimedia
(800) 903-5040

Edmark
(800) 426-0856

EduQuest/IBM
(800) 426-4968

Fairfield Language Technologies
(800) 788-0822

Great Wave Software
(800) 423-1144

Grolier Electronic Publishing
(800) 356-5590

Intellimation
(800) 346-8355

Interplay Productions
(714) 553-6678

Jump Music
(800) 289-5867

Knowledge Adventure (Davidson)
(800) 545-7677

Lawrence Productions
(616) 665-7075

The Learning Company
(800) 852-2255

Macmillan/McGraw-Hill
(860) 678-1212

EDUCATIONAL SOFTWARE PUBLISHERS *(cont.)*

MECC (order from Learning Co.)
(800) 852-2255

Microsoft Corporation
(800) 426-9400

Mindscape
(800) 283-8499

Misty City Software
(206) 820-2219

National Geographic Educational Services
(800) 368-2728

Optical Data Corporation
(800) 248-8478

Orange Cherry/New Media Schoolhouse
(914) 764-4104

Queue, Inc.
(800) 232-2224

Rand McNally
(800) 678-7263

Roger Wagner Publishing
(800) 497-3778

Scholastic, Inc.
(800) 541-5513

Sunburst Communications
(800) 321-7511

Teacher Support Software
(800) 228-2871

International Thomson Publishing
(800) 354-9706

Tom Snyder Productions
(800) 342-0236

Troll Micro
(800) 526-5289

Videodiscovery
(800) 548-3472

GLOSSARY

A

ASCII: American Standard Code for Information Interchange
assessment: evaluating a product
AUP (acceptable use policy): a document outlining terms and conditions for use of the Internet, signed by parents, students, and teachers
AVI: audio video interleaved—Microsoft's video format for *Windows*

B

bit: binary digit—a transistor or capacitor in a memory cell
BMP: (*Windows* graphic) bitmap; graphics file format
bookmark: option to mark a site location on the Internet
boot: to start a computer (Warm boot restarts a computer without turning it off; cold boot starts a computer from an off state.)
browser: application software which allows user to navigate the World Wide Web (ex., *Netscape*)
bulletin board (BBS): area on the Internet for the user to exchange information with other participants
button: in a multimedia program an object you create to allow action and/or movement to another area of the presentation
byte: 8 bits=1 byte; holds the equivalent of a single character

C

CD-ROM: compact disk-read only memory
clip art: prepared artwork or graphics to cut and paste
clipboard: area in program that holds graphics or text which has been cut or copied
copy: option to duplicate information on clipboard until pasted
CPU: central processing system—brains of the computer
crash: unexpected failure of equipment
cut: option to remove information from document and store on clipboard until pasted

D

default: settings already made in computer programs and on hardware
dialog box: window on the screen from which you make choices
digital camera: camera used to take pictures which are digitized for use on a computer program
DOS: disk operating system
download: to retrieve information, data, files, or pictures from an outside source

E

e-mail (electronic mail): usually brief messages sent and received over computer networks
edit: to make corrections/additions to a document
Ethernet: local area network card in computers connecting them together with cables

F

fax (facsimile): a document transmitted over the telephone via fax machine
font: style of type
format: prepare a disk in platform specific to read or write information
freeware: freely shared, copied, or given software
FTP (file transfer protocol): method of downloading Internet files

G

GIF: graphics interchange format—a graphics format often used for pictures transmitted by modem
GOPHER: Internet software that allows you to look through all kinds of online information
graphics: pictures and images

H

hardware: equipment or peripherals
home page: usually the first page at a World Wide Web site
hot buttons: shortcuts for performing actions (ex., Control-S is shortcut for saving.)
HTML (hypertext markup language): World Wide Web programming language
hypertext/hyperlink: in a document or Internet site, highlighted graphic or word which when clicked on will link you to another location

GLOSSARY *(cont.)*

I

icon: pictures on the screen representing files or programs
import: bring information into a document from another location
Internaut: Internet user
Internet service provider (ISP): company/organization providing access to the Internet

J

JPEG: Joint Photographic Experts Group

K

K: kilo = 1,000 (ex., 64 kilobytes or 64,000 bytes)

L

listserv: service a user joins which posts information from members of this service
log on: to sign onto a computer system

M

MOV: a video format
MPEG: an acronym for moving picture expert group: a video format
multimedia: computer presentation that involves images, movies, audio, etc., or a combination of all of the above

N

navigate: move around the Internet
netiquette: conduct rules for Internet use
network: group of connected computers

O

online: means a computer user is connected to the Internet

P

PCX: a bitmapped graphic file format, originally developed for the PC Paintbrush program
peripheral: external device connected to the computer (ex., printer)
PICT: (PICTure) MacIntosh graphics file format (PC version is .PCT)
platform: operating system such as Mac or DOS
public domain: freeware, software available to anyone

Q

***QuickTime*:** software product required to be installed on your computer to run movies

S

search engine: program used to search for information on the Internet (ex., *Yahoo*)
shareware: software which must be purchased after a limited trial period
software: programs/materials used on hardware
surfing: browse about on the Internet

T

telecommunications: communicating with other computers via modem
template: framework that has been prepared and can be completed and Saved As
text: data in the form of words or numbers
text box: space on the card where text can be typed
TIFF: tagged image file format, a graphics file format
transitions: ways to move from one card to another
trash/recycle bin: ways to get rid of unwanted information

U

undo: reverses the last action taken
upgrade: install newer, usually more powerful, software

V

virtual reality: computer simulated environment which appears to be real
virus: software program which intentionally sabotages another program, computer, or network

W

WAV: windows sound file (one minute of sound = 644 K to 5 mg)
World Wide Web (WWW): a system of html pages which are interconnected via hyperlinks

CITING ELECTRONIC SOURCES

Whether they are researching for projects or reports, your students need to cite all the resources in which they find usable information. There are printed guidelines for citing books and periodicals, but they must also cite electronic sources such as CD-ROM encyclopedias or reference materials and online sources of information. The following are some basic structures of those bibliography entries.

CD-ROM databases:

Author. "Title of Article." Title of Work. Type of Medium, version. Place of Publication: Publisher, date.

Electronic mail (e-mail):

Sender of e-mail message (e-mail address). "Subject of e-mail." Recipient (recipient's e-mail address). Date of message.

Internet sources (World Wide Web address):

Author. Title of item (or Web page). [Online] Available http://address/filename, date of download or document creation, if available.

Online interview or presentation by speaker:

Name of online speaker. [Online] Available software type: site address, date of session.

Online images, video clips, sound files:

Description of file. [Online Image (or Video Clip or Sound)] Available http://address/filename, date of download or document creation if available.

Web Links:

Classroom Connect: How to Cite Internet Resources
http://www.classroom.com/resource/citingnetresources.asp

Electronic Sources: MLA Style of Citation
http://www.uvm.edu/~ncrane/estyles/mla.html

Electronic Sources: APA Style of Citation
http://www.uvm.edu/~ncrane/estyles/apa.html

Citing Electronic Sources from the Library of Congress
http://memory.loc.gov/ammem/ndlpedu/cite.html

BIBLIOGRAPHY AND ADDITIONAL RESOURCES

Adams, Marian and Marsha Lifter. *Integrating Technology into the Curriculum: Primary.* Teacher Created Materials, 1997.

Bryant, Mary Helen. *Integrating Technology into the Curriculum.* Teacher Created Materials, 1996.

Dockterman, David. *Cooperative Learning and Technology.* Tom Snyder Productions, 1998.

Dockterman, David. *Great Teaching in the One-Computer Classroom.* Tom Snyder Productions, 1997.

Gardner, Paul. *Internet for Teachers and Parents.* Teacher Created Materials, 1996.

Gardner, Paul. *Managing Technology in the Middle School Classroom.* Teacher Created Materials, 1996.

Haag, Tim. *Internet for Kids.* Teacher Created Materials, 1996

Hayes, Deborah Shepherd. *Managing Technology in the Classroom.* Teacher Created Materials, 1995.

Hooper, Debi. *Integrating Technology into the Science Curriculum.* Teacher Created Materials, 1999.

Hooper, Debi. *Web Buddy: Software, Instructions, and Projects.* Teacher Created Materials, 1999.

Kopp, Kathleen. *Internet Activities for Social Studies.* Teacher Created Materials, 1998.

Sherwood, Walter. *Internet Activities for Math.* Teacher Created Materials, 1998.

Soares, Dennis. *Integrating Technology in the Math Curriculum.* Teacher Created Materials, 1998.

________. *Choices, Choices.* Tom Snyder Productions, 1997.

________. *Decisions, Decisions.* Tom Snyder Productions, 1997.

________. *Educational Software Preview Guide.* Educational Software Consortium, 1998.

________. *Fizz & Martina's Math Adventures.* Tom Snyder Productions, 1998.

________. *Graph Club.* Tom Snyder Productions, 1996–1998.

________. *Knowledge Adventure Spring Catalog.* Knowledge Adventure, 1998.

________. *National Inspirer.* Tom Snyder Productions, 1998.

________. *PrimeTime Math.* Tom Snyder Productions, 1997.

________. *Rainforest Researchers.* Tom Snyder Productions, 1996.

________. *Science Court.* Tom Snyder Productions, 1997.

________. *Best of Internet Activities The,.* Teacher Created Materials, 1999.

________. *TimeLiner.* Tom Snyder Productions, 1995.